Cambridge Elements

Elements in Environmental Humanities
edited by
Louise Westling
University of Oregon
Serenella Iovino
University of North Carolina at Chapel Hill
Timo Maran
University of Tartu

GROWING HOPE

Narratives of Food Justice

Alexa Weik von Mossner
University of Klagenfurt

Shaftesbury Road, Cambridge CB2 8EA, United Kingdom

One Liberty Plaza, 20th Floor, New York, NY 10006, USA

477 Williamstown Road, Port Melbourne, VIC 3207, Australia

314–321, 3rd Floor, Plot 3, Splendor Forum, Jasola District Centre,
New Delhi – 110025, India

103 Penang Road, #05–06/07, Visioncrest Commercial, Singapore 238467

Cambridge University Press is part of Cambridge University Press & Assessment,
a department of the University of Cambridge.

We share the University's mission to contribute to society through the pursuit of
education, learning and research at the highest international levels of excellence.

www.cambridge.org
Information on this title: www.cambridge.org/9781009500579

DOI: 10.1017/9781009500555

When citing this work, please include a reference to the DOI 10.1017/9781009500555

First published 2025

A catalogue record for this publication is available from the British Library

ISBN 978-1-009-50057-9 Hardback
ISBN 978-1-009-50059-3 Paperback
ISSN 2632-3125 (online)
ISSN 2632-3117 (print)

Growing Hope

Narratives of Food Justice

Elements in Environmental Humanities

DOI: 10.1017/9781009500555
First published online: January 2025

Alexa Weik von Mossner
University of Klagenfurt

Author for correspondence: Alexa Weik von Mossner,
Alexa.WeikvonMossner@aau.at

Abstract: *Growing Hope* takes a closer look at how such narratives can carry the promise of a better future in the face of grim realities. It brings together two kinds of narratives that are rarely considered in conjunction: stories about urban community gardening and stories about vegan food justice. It shows that there is much common ground between these movements and that the stories told by them are worth exploring as part of a larger narrative about creating a better and more equitable future. In the United States, this is especially true for the stories told by and about people of color and their historically marginalized communities. Employing an econarratological approach informed by critical food studies, environmental justice ecocriticism and transmedia studies, *Growing Hope* explores a selection of narratives about people who fight against food injustice and the ideologies sustaining it: stories about defiant gardening and culinary self-empowerment.

Keywords: Food justice, urban community gardening, narrative, Hope, vegan

ISBNs: 9781009500579 (HB), 9781009500593 (PB), 9781009500555 (OC)
ISSNs: 2632-3125 (online), 2632-3117 (print)

Contents

Introduction

Hope appears to be in short supply these days as we begin to face the devastating consequences of the unsustainable industries and inequitable lifestyles still common in much of the industrialized world. There are now so many interlocking crises – from climate change, deforestation, and species extinction to plastic pollution, ocean acidification, soil degradation, and food insecurity – that it can feel overwhelming just to try to keep track of all of them, let alone tackle their causes. Against this backdrop, calls for empowering and hope-inducing narratives have been multiplying in recent years (Painter 2020; Paoletta 2023; Strazds 2019), but it remains unclear who can provide them or how they might be cultivated and put into practice. There are many possible answers to these questions, which depend in part on the underlying understanding of hope (Schmid Callina et al. 2018) and its relation to transformative action (Mauch 2019; Ojala 2023). In *Growing Hope*, I want to focus on a selection of food justice narratives I have become interested in because they touch on so many of the problems we face, and because they aim to grow hope through transformative embodied action while also exposing local and global inequity and addressing intergenerational and interspecies ethics. I will argue that such narratives are very much needed if we are to imagine ways out of the ongoing ecological and social polycrisis and find ways to move forward.

The interdisciplinary field of food justice research "seeks to understand how inequalities of race, class and gender are reproduced and contested within food systems" (Glennie & Alkon 2018) and recognizes that the agricultural industrial complex exploits humans, animals, and ecosystems. Despite tremendous gains in productivity in industrial agriculture, over 300 million people worldwide are facing high levels of acute food insecurity (Carruth 2013; World Food Programme 2024) and millions more only have access to food that lacks nutrients (Penniman 2018). The industry's carbon emissions, amounting to about 10 percent of greenhouse gases (EPA), are further exacerbating global food injustice through climate-related forms of "slow violence" (Nixon 2011) such as drought conditions and torrential rain, which affect agriculture in countries that are not among the top emitters of greenhouse gases. Food justice scholars demand that we must "shed light on the symptoms of unjust access to food within the food system, while simultaneously bringing attention to the insidious causes of these problems" (Agyeman & McEntee 2014, 211), which are rooted in global food commodification and neoliberal deregulation. Food cooperatives and food sovereignty movements, which support small farmers as well as local food systems within and outside of large urban centers, have arisen in opposition to this regime, offering what Philip McMichael (2002, 2009) calls "food from somewhere" to contest the invisible bulk of the "food from nowhere" regime that marks globalized industrial food supply (Campbell 2015). However, given the pervasive economic, cultural, and legal power behind that supply, such resistance is an uphill battle.

One goal of food justice narratives is to expose such structural inequalities, along with the capitalist ideologies which sustain them, and which threaten the well-being of local communities and entire ecosystems. However, it would be a mistake to stop there. "As important as it is to expose the wrongs that are embedded within our food system," write Paul Stock, Michael Carolan, and Christopher Rosin in *Food Utopias* (2015, 220), "it is also imperative that we share our visions of what a better system would be." Hugh Campbell has drawn attention to "two interesting polarities in our political relationship with food" (2015, 195). One of these poles "orients food politics around the project of making bad food dynamics more visible . . . . The other pole orients around how to make better food practices more thinkable" (195). I am interested in both these poles but will emphasize the second, looking at narratives that depict some of the practices people are engaging in to feed themselves in defiance of adverse circumstances while "imagining new ecological and social relationships" (Alkon & Agyeman 2011, 18). It is for this forward-looking pole of food justice activism that hope as a lived practice is so very crucial.

According to psychologists Kristina Schmid Callina et al., hope is "fundamental for understanding human flourishing" (Schmid Callina 2017, 9) and is marked by three necessary ingredients: "positive future expectations, agency, and trust" (10). Why these ingredients are relevant in combination becomes immediately obvious when we consider the existential act of growing food. As food activist and farmer Ashoka Finely puts it in Todd Darling's documentary *Occupy the Farm* (2012), "it's inherently hopeful to plant a seed because you hope that it grows, you hope that you can harvest it." The hope for a good harvest entails positive future expectations as well as the agency to put the actual seeds in the ground (which necessitates access to both seeds and ground), along with the trust that all the effort and investment will pay off in the end – that the crop will not be destroyed by some kind of pest or weather event. However, what happens if such agency is *restricted*, and trust *destroyed* due to historical, sociopolitical, or environmental causes? Is hope still possible under such conditions? Jonathan Lear has famously argued that the Crow nation developed a form of "radical hope" when faced with the destruction of its traditional tribal ways with the advance of Whites across the Great Plains (2006, 103). Understood in this way, radical hope entails "the positive expectations for which one hopes" outstripping "one's conceptual or imaginative abilities" (Schmid Callina et al. 2017, 20). Mosley et al. (2020) have proposed four pathways to it: (a) understanding the history of oppression along with the actions of resistance taken to transform these conditions, (b) embracing ancestral pride, (c) envisioning equitable possibilities, and (d) creating meaning and purpose in life by adopting an orientation to social justice. We will see that all four pathways have been used in American food justice narratives, in which protagonists must often fall back on radical hope because their agency to bring about what they have been hoping for is curtailed. Not all of those stories have happy endings, but the narratives I have selected here tend to project a *sense of possibility* and what Henry Mitchell has called "the defiance of gardeners" (1985, 1): a refusal to give up in the face of overwhelming odds.[1] It is a form of defiance that can be useful not only in local food justice struggles but also in the stories we tell each other during the long fight for a just, equitable, and ecologically sustainable future.

Growing Hope brings together two kinds of food justice narratives that are rarely considered in conjunction: stories about urban community gardening projects and stories about vegan food justice. Although certainly not all community gardeners are vegans, and not all vegans are gardeners, I will show that there is much common ground between these movements. In the United States, which will be my focal point, this is especially true for food justice narratives told by people of color and by other communities that have been historically denied food security (Murphy & Mook 2022).[2] As food justice scholars Sandy Brown and Christy Getz have noted, "food security is more than an individual or household condition to be scientifically measured, but rather a lens through which to consider the highly unequal, uneven dynamics of global agricultural production, trade, and consumption" (2011, 164–165). Such dynamics have been shown to be closely intertwined with the social repercussions of climate change (Gregory, Ingram, & Brklacich 2005; Wheeler & von Braun 2013), especially for communities in densely populated urban and peri-urban areas (Lucertini & Di Giustino 2021). This is particularly relevant in the socio-economic geography of the United States, where food deserts affecting the poorest parts of urban populations often coincide with heat-trapping concrete jungles and less tree cover (Zhang et al. 2022). Research has also shown that access is not the only determining factor in healthy eating habits, but that cultural factors play an important role

---

[1] Following the lead of narratologists such as Jan-Noël Thon (2016) and Marie Laure Ryan (2004), I will transfer narratological work done in one medium to another since there is no reason to confine narratological work to one medium if we are mindful of the specific affordances of media forms and channels.

[2] Food security, as defined by the U.S. Department of Agriculture, means always having access to enough food for an active, healthy life for all household members (www.ers.usda.gov/topics/food-nutrition-assistance/food-security-in-the-u-s). In the definition of the Food and Agriculture Organization of the United Nations, it is "a situation that exists when all people, at all times, have physical, social and economic access to sufficient, safe and nutritious food that meets their dietary needs and food preferences for an active and healthy life" (1996).

(Dubowitz et al. 2015). It is through this lens of food security and (vegan) food justice that I will explore a selection of stories about people who fight for the right to grow, sell, and eat food that is "fresh, nutritious, affordable, culturally appropriate, and grown locally with care for the well-being of the land, workers, and animals" (Alkon & Agyeman 2011, 18) – stories about defiant gardening and culinary self-empowerment in a variety of genres and media that range from personal reflections, critical essays, autobiographies, and cookbooks to blogs, videos, and documentaries.

My theoretical approach to these nonfiction narratives is rooted in the econarratological work I first developed in *Affective Ecologies* (2017), and it is informed by several research fields relevant to my inquiry, among them food justice studies, vegan studies, environmental justice ecocriticism, ecomedia studies, and transmedial narratology. Ecocritic Ursula Heise has noted that, historically, narrative theory has mostly focused on everyday conversational storytelling, on the one hand, and on "highly elaborate fictional storytelling" on the other, pointing out that neither of these modes of theorization works unproblematically with "story templates that cut across fiction and nonfiction in environmental texts" (2020, 204). Empirical research has shown that there is not much of a difference in how audiences respond to fiction and nonfiction (Malecki et al. 2019), and my own scholarship has always cut across that divide. Yet in what follows, I deliberately focus on nonfiction because I am interested in how such narratives both depict and aim to grow radical hope in relation to ongoing real-world struggles for food justice. A central question is the degree of *narrative agency* afforded by different media forms, and how claiming such agency can amplify a strategy that the vegan chef Bryant Terry has formulated as follows: "*Start with the visceral to ignite the cerebral and end at the political*" (2009, 318; emphasis in original). Since much of my research over the past years has been dedicated to precisely this trajectory from an audience's emotional response to their cognitive processing and the political dimensions that such engagements might have, I am especially interested in the role of narrative agency in this process.

As a concept, narrative agency refers to the ability to control the development of a story and to navigate narrative environments (van Laer & Orazi 2023). Hanna Meretoja has argued that it "shifts the focus to *action*, to ways of acting and affecting the world," and that it should be understood as "the ability to use, interpret and reinterpret the narratives that are culturally available to us, to analyze and challenge them, and to make choices of how to narrate our lives and relationships and the world around us" (2018, 11).[3] A crucial dimension of

---

[3] According to van Laer and Orazi, narrative agency refers to the ability to control the development of a story and to navigate narrative environments (2023).

narratives, in this definition, is that they "shape our abilities to imagine different possibilities of thought, affect, and action" (12). I will show that looking at American food justice narratives across a variety of media can give us a better understanding of the role of narrative agency in affecting sustainable social change in a society where the (lack of) access to healthy food continues to be circumscribed by structural inequalities. My analysis will start from more traditional media such as documentary film, which often takes an observational stance, and then move toward more digital and transmedial forms of nonfiction storytelling that make it easier for individuals and communities to speak for themselves. According to Henry Jenkins's influential definition, "a transmedia story unfolds across multiple media platforms, with each new text making a distinctive and valuable contribution to the whole" (2006, 95). It is marked by multiple entry points, an expansive storyworld, narrative depth, and active audience participation. Most research in transmedia studies focuses on fictional storyworlds and mainstream entertainment media, but there are storytellers who want more than entertain (Molony 2014).[4] Particularly relevant are the narrative strategies of *transmedia activism*, which uses "the capabilities of transmedia to amplify underrepresented voices and make stories that suggest a more inclusive future" (Hancox 2021). Such voices have innovated nonfiction transmedia storytelling about issues around food justice by illuminating the relationship between people, places, and practices to affect social change.

Part I of *Growing Hope* – "Grow: Visions of Defiant Gardening" – looks at stories of community gardening in the middle of urban food deserts in Los Angeles and the Bay Area. Chapter 1, "Narrating Resistance," approaches the hopes inherent in urban farming projects along with their fragility through the lenses of two documentaries that frame them as a form of resistance. Scott Hamilton Kennedy's *The Garden* (2008) chronicles the rise and fall of the South Central Farm in Los Angeles and portrays some of the people who fought for its survival. Todd Darling's *Occupy the Farm* (2014) tells a similar story about the struggle over UC Berkeley's Gill Tract Farm in Albany; however, the fact that both the protagonists and the antagonists in this film have ties to one of the most prestigious land-grant universities not only affects their respective levels of (narrative) agency but also the outcome of the story. Chapter 2, "Projecting Resilience," focuses on the depiction of defiant farming and radical hope in the postindustrial space of Detroit. It approaches the diverse community of farmers that grow food in the city's countless abandoned lots via Mark MacInnis's documentary *Urban Roots* (2011). The second part of the chapter considers the negotiation of narrative agency in Bridget Besaw's documentary project

---

[4] For a sustained narratological discussion of the storyworld concept, see Herman (2009).

Rooted about Germaine Jenkins's Fresh Future Farm in Atlanta, and in Marc Decena's *Farming while Black* (2023), a film based on Leah Penniman's influential book (2018) of the same title and featuring Penniman as protagonist.

Part II – "Eat: Narrating Vegan Food Justice" – explores the growing hope that a reduction of animal consumption might change the morally untenable and ecologically disastrous status quo, which makes millions of Americans unhealthy and involves the breeding and killing of seventy billion land animals per year for human consumption (Holmes 2021, 172). Although veganism continues to be largely overlooked as a rights-based social justice movement in the interests of both human and nonhuman animals (178), the authors of the vegan food justice narratives I will consider reject not only the Standard American Diet (SAD) as calorie-dense, nutrient-poor, and sickening, but also the notion that veganism is inherently white and elitist.[5] Using frameworks of intersectionality and decolonization, they reimagine veganism as a way for people of color to move toward personal and community empowerment and a path toward an understanding of food justice that goes beyond the human and the current historical moment.

Chapter 3, "Decolonizing Veganism," starts from A. Breeze Harper's ground-breaking anthology *Sistah Vegan* (2010), which collects the personal stories of Black vegan women aiming to decolonize their bodies from heavily processed and harmful diets, and then considers the ways in which the Ko sisters negotiate anti-speciesism and Black liberation in their co-written book of essays *Aphro-ism* (2017). The second part of the chapter turns to Jasmine Leyva's documentary film *The Invisible Vegan* (2019), which combines Leyva's own personal journey toward veganism as a young Black woman with a more general look at the adverse health implications of a traditional Soul Food diet with its staple dishes of collard greens, fried chicken, mac-n-cheese, and black-eyed peas, and an interrogation of veganism from the perspective of Black men. Chapter 4, "Visceralizing Food Justice," explores the work of Black vegan nutritionists, food bloggers, and social media influencers before turning to the transmedial storytelling of Bryant Terry, a Black vegan chef, food justice activist, educator, and author who hopes that his work will empower people "to cook at home and share meals with family and friends as a revolutionary first step toward food justice" (2009, 2). I will look at how Terry uses his recipes, books, videos, and artwork toward this goal.

The Afterword returns to the notion of radical hope, along with more global and planetary concerns. Narratives about community gardening and vegan food justice not only promote ways of being in the world that can improve physical

---

[5] The omnivore but meat-focused SAD consists mostly of refined and processed "fast food," soft drinks, and packaged snacks (Grotto & Zied 2010, 603).

and emotional health, but they may also have the potential to help reduce the weight of people's ecological footprint on the planet. As Erinn Gilson and Sarah Kenehan suggest, "we might respond to climate change by amending environmental and agricultural practices not only with the aim of reducing emissions and mitigating the effects of climate change but also with the aim of generating more sustainable and just – that is, democratic – food systems" (2018, 2). It is in this way that food justice narratives can also help address climate anxiety and other emotions we experience at this moment of great ecological uncertainty. There is a visceral, embodied component to all of them that helps us understand that people *are* changing things for themselves and their communities, and that we have in fact the (narrative) agency to become active ourselves. As John Holloway has put it, "It is the very horror of the world that obliges us to learn hope" (2005, 8). Narratives of food justice might just teach us.

GROW: VISIONS OF DEFIANT GARDENING

1 Narrating Resistance

One of the most memorable moments in Scott Hamilton Kennedy's documentary feature *The Garden* (2003) is a series of aerial shots. Placed early in the film and after a montage that gives us more bounded glimpses of the South Central Farm, the bird's eye view shows the impressive size of what, during the twelve years of its existence, was the United States's largest urban community garden. The camera travels above the fourteen acres of lush green: densely planted crops covering the ground and mature fruit trees towering above them. From here, the film cuts to another aerial shot, and then another, each one higher up and farther away, revealing the surrounding area of South Los Angeles: warehouses, parking lots, streets, and wrecking yards, framed by one of the nation's principal railroad lines and a busy six-lane viaduct. From the stunning vista of this veritable oasis in a concrete desert, the film cuts to black and its title: *The Garden*.[6] Even for viewers unaware that two years before the film's release, "bulldozers razed the South Central Farm" (Emmett 2016, 165), the sequence conveys a sense of vulnerability, of encroachment.

In *Cultivating Environmental Justice*, Robert Emmett reminds us of the "fragility of community gardens" in densely populated urban spaces (2016, 3). According to the Soil Science Society of America (SSSA), a community garden is a versatile green space that "can be urban, suburban, or rural," it can consist of one large

---

[6] In 2003, the Los Angeles City Council voted to change South Central Los Angeles to South Los Angeles in an effort to rebuild communities after the Los Angeles 1992 Uprising. Many members of the communities still call the area South Central, however, and ignore or reject the official renaming.

community plot or several individual plots, and it "can grow flowers, vegetables – or community" (2024). The one featured in *The Garden* grows all three and is called both a farm and a garden by the people who have planted it. Such terminological inexactitudes are not uncommon, but we will see that they can matter a great deal when it comes to the long-term survival of an urban agriculture project. While they share several features with private backyard gardens and commercial urban farms, community gardens tend to be marked by a focus on the communities that care for them (Raneng, Howes & Pickering 2023).[7] Emmett links them to the long struggle for environmental justice in the United States, pointing to dozens of community garden leaders who "have engaged gardening as an aesthetic and ethical practice that joins social and environmental concerns" (4).[8] The SSSA suggests we might think about such gardens as "community-managed open spaces" (2024) which can help combat food insecurity. In the United States, their history spans from the "Pingree's Potato Patches" program in nineteenth-century Detroit to the "liberty gardens" and "victory gardens" during World War I and II and their more recent resurgence in response to multiple social and ecological crises (Smithsonian Gardens 2024). Emmett notes that, historically, such gardens "appeared in times of need and public demand, only to be built over in a pattern of bust-and-boom real estate development and urban economics over the course of the twentieth century" (2018, 134). Because of competing interests and the uneven distribution of agency among various stakeholders, community gardens tend to depend on economic cycles and related effects of decapitalization, gentrification, and recapitalization of urban space (Alkon & Cadji 2020; Glowa 2017). They also depend on people willing to invest their time in the maintenance of a garden – and on other people considering that a meaningful investment. Hence their inevitable fragility.

That a diverse and mostly low-income urban area like South (Central) Los Angeles became the site of the largest community garden in the United States is meaningful precisely because its majority Latinx and Black inhabitants were (and still are) lacking access to fresh fruit and vegetables. In their introduction to *Cultivating Food Justice*, Alison Hope Alkon and Julian Agyeman remind us that "race and class play a central role in organizing the production, distribution, and consumption of food. Time and again, communities of color have been subject to laws and policies that have taken away their ability to own and

---

[7] According to the NYU Urban Farm Lab, "farming as a practice is a larger investment than gardening . . . . Gardening is a more sedentary activity that has neither the level of planning" that marks commercially oriented farming, "nor severity of goal. The average gardener goes about his duties as a chore rather than a necessity and as such distinguishes his or herself from the farmer" (2014).

[8] American writers have popularized ideas around the uses of urban gardens for individual well-being and ecological sustainability (Pollan 1991), along with the concept of a "rambunctious" nature that is thriving along their edges (Marris 2011).

manage land for food production" (2011, 17). Members of these communities have been exploited as farm laborers; others live in densely populated urban spaces marked by an abundance of liquor stores and a lack of access to both green space and fresh vegetables. So-called "food deserts," explains geographer Michael Widener, are "regions in which access to food retailers that stock fresh, affordable, and healthy food options are lacking or nonexistent" (2018, 257). When supermarkets pull out of neighborhoods because they are no longer profitable, the people left behind are forced to travel long distances to the next grocery store, or they are stuck with buying their food at convenience stores. The opportunity to grow one's own vegetables is quite literally a lifesaver in such urban spaces, but food justice activists are critical of the desert metaphor, preferring the term "food apartheid" instead to reflect the structural injustices and disparities in food access faced by low-income communities and communities of color.[9]

Coined by the Black farmer-activist Karen Washington, the term food apartheid draws attention to the "root causes of inequity in our food system based on race, class, and geography," emphasizing that "healthy, fresh food is accessible in wealthy neighborhoods while unhealthy food abounds in poor neighborhoods." Speaking of food apartheid rather than using the geographical metaphor of the desert underscores that this structural inequity "results from decades of discriminatory planning and policy decisions" (Washington quoted in Walker 2023) and thus allocates agency. As Leah Penniman explains, the notion of apartheid makes clear that there is "a human-created system of segregation" in the U.S. "that relegates certain groups to food opulence and prevents others from accessing life-giving nourishment" (2018, 4). Given these inequities, it is no wonder that for the affected communities growing one's own food is not only an existential need but also an embodied way of claiming agency and staving off anger and despair. Philosopher David Cooper suggests that four virtues are "induced by any kind of gardening: care and respect for life, structure and routine, humility, and hope" (2008, 96). Yet disenfranchised communities creating farms and gardens hope to bring about more than just a good harvest.

It is the South Central Farmers' radical hope that their actions will bring about environmental and food justice for their community that makes *The Garden* such a powerful film. In the wake of its critical success, which included an Academy Award nomination for Best Documentary Feature, a slate of other documentaries on urban agriculture projects was released, among them Dan Susman's *Growing Cities* (2013), Roman Zenz's *Urban Fruit* (2013), Andrew Hasse's *Edible City*

---

[9] As Jo Walker points out, "the physical conditions creating a desert ecosystem are natural whereas food deserts result from historical injustices that have perpetuated inequities within our food system" (2023).

(2014), Karney Hatch's *Plant this Movie* (2014), and, more recently, Rachel Caccese's *Urban Farmers* (2020). These films highlight many of the benefits of urban community gardening for people, neighborhoods, and the nonhuman world. However, despite their efforts to showcase diverse communities, they lack the sustained attention to environmental and food injustice that marks *The Garden*. Although it lost the Oscar to Simon Chinn and James Marsh's *Man on Wire* (2008), the media buzz surrounding the coveted nomination helped bring to international attention the film's dramatic story about community resistance and celebrity support. As Jennifer Catsoulis quips in her blistering review of *The Garden* for the *New York Times*, it "has all the elements of a John Sayles drama: hard-working immigrants, self-serving politicians, a greedy land developer and Daryl Hannah" (2009).[10] In a much more nuanced approach, media studies scholar Jean Retzinger has noted that Kennedy's documentary "both draws upon and departs from Hollywood movies" (2011, 237) in that it positions the filmmaker "as a trusted observer, granted access to private moments" by the real-world people it portrays – a group that includes Daryl Hannah, who appears as herself. My own analysis of how these elements provide a structure for viewers' engagement in the protagonists' struggle for environmental and food justice will draw on cognitive film theory and put *The Garden* in conversation with another nonfiction film, Todd Darling's *Occupy the Farm* (2014), which has a similar subject, approach, and plotline, but is also a powerful reminder that the outcomes of food justice struggles depend not least on the financial means, social capital, and (narrative) agency of the stakeholders involved.

Food Justice and Narrative Agency: Scott Hamilton Kennedy's *The Garden*

The story of the South Central Farm started long before there even was a garden with another remarkable fight for environmental justice: in 1986, the fourteen-acre tract in an area zoned for industrial and residential uses was acquired by eminent domain for $4.8 million by the City of Los Angeles for the establishment of a trash incinerator. One year later, the project was stopped by the Concerned Citizens of South Central led by the Black community organizer Juanita Tate (Woo 2004).[11] Five years later and under the impression of the 1992 Los Angeles Uprising, the LA Harbor Department granted the regional

---

[10] In 2011, the film was the subject of an entire special issue of the journal *Environmental Communication*, and over the years, ecocritics have continued to engage with the film (e.g., Emmett 2016; Fiskio 2012).

[11] Environmental justice fights have often been led by Black women. The 1982 protests against the construction of a hazardous-waste center in Warren County, NC are regarded an important catalyst of the movement (Bullard 1990).

Food Bank a revocable permit to use the tract for a community garden.[12] After an initial cleanup, over 360 Latinx families created what Teresa Mares and Devon Peña call "a veritable Mesoamerican agroecological landscape in the inner city." Filling the tract with local crops and "ancient heirloom seeds of landrace *maíz, calabacita,* and *frijol,*" the South Central Farmers replicated "the *huerto familiar* or hometown kitchen gardens in Mexico, Central America, Puerto Rico, Cuba, or the Dominican Republic" (Mares & Peña 2010, 244–245), thus ensuring food sovereignty and community resilience. Popularized by the international peasant movement *La Vía Campesina* as a rights-based counter-vision to neoliberal economics, the idea of food sovereignty insists on peoples' rights to define their own agriculture policies and promotes a model of small-scale sustainable agriculture (Witman, Desmarais & Wiebe 2010).[13] Interrogating the concept through the lens of critical utopianism, Nave Wald argues that it can function as a hopeful alternative to the status quo: "it challenges the corporatist agro-industry model, but it goes much further in arguing for a radical transformation of both food production and of the social and political relations of food production, distribution and consumption" (2015, 110). For the South Central Farm, it ended abruptly when the previous owner of the tract, the developer Ralph Horowitz, sued the City of Los Angeles for the third time because the land was used for nonpublic purposes, constituting a breach of contract. After two failed attempts, Horowitz reached a settlement that allowed him to buy back the land for five million dollars, a price vastly below its current value. Weeks later, in January 2004, the farmers received an eviction notice.

For Kennedy, this was the moment when he got involved as a filmmaker. He did not have time to write a script or prepare for the shoot when he learned about the eviction scheduled for February 29, 2004. A friend of his had seen a PBS feature about the South Central Farm and talked about potentially making a movie, but when the eviction notice hit and the farmers announced their resistance, Kennedy went there immediately and started filming the story as it unfolded, trusting that he would be able to fill in the conflict's backstory with archival footage and interviews (Poland 2010). It would turn out to be a three-year commitment during which he developed a close relationship with some of the farmers that became crucial for the structure of *The Garden*, which "keeps their words and voices in dialogic engagement" (Enck-Wanzer 2011, 366) with

---

12 The 1992 Los Angeles Uprising erupted after the acquittal of four white LAPD officers charged with the beating of the Black motorist Rodney King and had detrimental consequences: "2,383 people were injured, 8,000 were arrested, 51 were killed, and over 700 businesses were burned" (Bergesen & Herman 1998, 39).

13 Jessica Clendenning et al. observe that "while many organizations do not use the language of food sovereignty explicitly, the motives behind urban food activism are similar across movements" (2015, 165).

Kennedy's own narrative agency as director. In the film, the story starts not with the first eviction notice but in the modest home of an elderly Latino man who is beginning his day, thus establishing a sense of "intimate proximity" (Retzinger 2011, 338). He leaves his house before dawn to take the bus and then opens the main gate to the South Central Farm for both the camera and the viewer. Music sets in and leads into a one-minute montage of colorful images, showing farmers at work and children at play, and ending with the series of aerial shots I discussed at the beginning of the chapter.

Cinematic space is not a coherent geographical area, explains Andreas Kretzer with reference to the work of French filmmaker and critic Éric Rohmer. Rather, it is composed by viewers in their imagination, aided by three types of fragments: "the space that is represented in the individual shot, the assembled space of the montage, and the spatial imagination stimulated by sound" (2021, 22). While this might be more obvious in fiction films, which are often shot in a variety of locations that only come together in the editing room and postproduction process to create the illusion of spatial continuity, it is also true for documentaries. If the first two types of fragments are most prominent in Kennedy's introductory montage as they evoke the lush expanse of the garden against its concrete surroundings, the third is important in the sequences preceding and following it, which foreground big city sounds that seem at odds with the green space. Another important dimension to the film's sound-scape is the constant presence of Spanish, often without accompanying sub-titles, which signals that it is the farmers' voices that are foregrounded in the film and that it is mostly Spanish-speaking people who are inhabiting the space of this community garden.

While the opening sequence establishes the centrality of its cinematic space, it is not a coincidence that the important "elements" that, according to Catsoulis, make *The Garden* comparable to a fiction film, are all *characters* ("hard-working immigrants, self-serving politicians, a greedy land developer and Daryl Hannah"). As the cognitive film scholar Carl Plantinga reminds us with reference to the ethics of representation, the characters of nonfiction films function in much the same ways as fictional ones, but with one important difference. When creating fictional characters, Plantinga notes, "I must be sensitive to questions of stereotyping . . . . But those obligations are to the communities to which I distribute my film," along with those who are repre-sented in it, not to the fictional characters themselves since they do not exist (2019, 120). The ethical obligations of a documentary filmmaker, by contrast, "extend to the people whose images and recorded voices I use" (121). Since the protagonists of a documentary such as *The Garden* are people who represent themselves and their own lives, it matters morally how they are represented

(Plantinga 2023, 9).[14] Of the over 360 people who worked on the South Central Farm when he started filming, Kennedy chose to focus on just a few who were at the forefront of resistance: Rufina Juarez and Tezozomoc, who had been elected by the farmers to save the garden, and Deacon Alexander, a former member of the Black Panthers. Other farmers shown in the film often speak Spanish to express their fear and distress, but these main protagonists use English as they claim narrative agency to influence the fate of the South Central Farm because, as Rufina puts it early in the film, "something just isn't right" with the eviction notice they have received. What she means by that is not explained at this point, but the film goes on to make an argument against the eviction on moral grounds.

The Garden's moral structure is tied closely to viewers' engagement with its protagonists. Plantinga notes that most "documentary filmmakers … encourage allegiances and antipathies [to characters] as a means of strengthening and providing a structure for the viewer's emotional involvement" (2019, 121). Kennedy aligns viewers with Rufina, Tezo, Deacon, and, to a lesser degree, the rest of the South Central Farmers by providing both "subjective access" and "spatio-temporal attachment" (Smith 2021, 142–186) to their subjectivity. The film invites viewers to build moral allegiance to them since it is their point of view that they share during its depiction of the three-year-long struggle to save the South Central Farm – from their moments of hope, strength, and confidence to the darker times when there is infighting, tears, and despair. Those who stand in the way of the farmers' fight for food justice and sovereignty are shown more briefly and with little access to their subjectivity. They either oppose the garden – such as Horowitz and Tate, who, as chairwoman of the Concerned Citizens of South Central, wants to establish a soccer field on a part of the tract – or they are seeming supporters who only pay lip service. The latter group includes the Black councilwoman Jan Perry, who makes alliances that serve her own interests, and LA City Council member Antonio Villaraigosa, who, once he is elected Mayor of Los Angeles, only "meekly states that he wishes there was more he could do to save the garden" (Starkman 2009). Even though they are given the opportunity to speak and present their views, these players are characterized by their lack of support for the South Central Farm and the farmers' moral claims on environmental and food justice, thus functioning as the film's antagonists. With reference to Hollywood movies, Murray Smith has argued that viewers' character allegiance and emotional response are guided by the overall moral structure of a given film, which may be "characterized by a spectrum of moral gradations"

---

[14] Plantinga explains that "from the standpoints of both rationalist and intuitionist accounts of moral learning, there is reason to hypothesize that screen stories can foster such learning" (2023, 9).

or binary in nature (2022, 190). *The Garden* demonstrates that such moral structuring works in the same way for documentaries.

Providing a moral structure for viewers' emotional engagement is particularly important for a film that revolves around a complicated and drawn-out legal battle that is not easy to understand. "The South Central farmers' arguments for their rights are not based on long-term inhabitation and property ownership," observes Janet Fiskio, "their grounds are their ability to feed themselves from the land and the community they have formed in this space" (2012, 317). As one of the farmers, Josefina, puts it in the film: "For me, it's the story of life. Because without the land, we are nothing. What are we without the land? Try to plant on cement and you'll get nothing. It's life, simply life." But even as they are not invested in ownership, the farmers are aware that its absence robs them of agency in their struggle for justice. "The only power we have right now is that lawsuit," the civil rights lawyer Dan Stormer tells the farmers after he has helped them achieve an injunction in court, "and that's a tenuous power." Viewers are invited to care not so much about who owns the land or what the legal situation is, but about the moral arguments of the farmers. "Battle lines are drawn between the pastoral and the industrial, the powerless and powerful, virtue and greed," as Retzinger has aptly observed (2011, 359). Food fittingly "serves as a means to mark and measure character" in this conflict, and the antagonists are all coming up short.

What is most remarkable about *The Garden*, however, is not that its characters could populate a John Sayles film, as Catsoulis has it, but that it features some turning points that might be considered too farfetched even for a Hollywood melodrama. The involvement of celebrities in the final weeks of the confrontation – a group that also includes Joan Baez, Martin Sheen, and Donald Glover – helps secure media attention and additional funds. After refusing to sell the land to the farmers during two years of struggle, Horowitz changes his mind and says he will do so for 16.3 million dollars, three times more than what he paid for it. With the help of their prominent allies, the farmers manage the seemingly impossible: they raise 16.3 million dollars, mostly from the Annenberg Foundation, no more than two days away from the eviction date. Horowitz, however, refuses to sell, going on record with the following statement: "Even if they raised a hundred million dollars, this group could not buy this property . . . [This is] not about money. It's about: I don't like their cause, and I don't like their conduct." He also claims that the farmers "don't speak English" and that they are mostly illegal immigrants who are "not really poor" because they sell some of the food they grow in their community garden. These claims are audible as a recording from Horowitz's court deposition, laying bare "his ethnocentrism and racism . . . in the presumption that the [f]armers are not American" (Enck-Wanzer 2011, 367). The most severe blow, however, is that he refuses to sell. It is the reversal of fortune we tend to find at the end of the second act in Hollywood films, the "all is lost" moment that squashes the hopes of the protagonist – only that in this case the script was written by judges, foundations, and landowners who possess vastly more narrative agency than the farmers.

From here, the film marches to its emotional climax: the forceful eviction on July 5, 2006. The sequence starts with the farmers' tense faces as they wait for the police to arrive. They keep a night watch, carrying candles, determined not to allow anyone to destroy their garden. When the police do show up the next morning, donning riot gear, helicopters circling above the farmers, some of them have chained themselves to the fence that surrounds the farm. Somber music plays as the camera once again lifts for an aerial shot, giving viewers one last view of the garden in all its glory. Then the music picks up pace, accompanied by the farmers' chanting. "I pay my tax," one of them screams her anguish into the faces of unimpressed policemen. "I'm old lady. How am I gonna survive now?" When the police cut the fence and go ahead with the eviction, it is brutal, not only because of their treatment of the people as they make arrests, but also because of what they do to the garden. Bulldozers rip it apart, leveling crops and killing the trees. Farmers rattle the fence screaming, sobbing, and watching helplessly. The soundtrack amplifies the noises of destruction and distress. It is over these images that Horowitz speaks again: "What they should have said to the taxpayers of Los Angeles, and to me, is: 'This is a gracious country, thank you very much for letting us have these gardens here. Thank you. *Thank you!*'" When it is finally over, Kennedy returns to the grieving farmers and leaves it to them to comment: "I remember the last words in the Pledge of Allegiance," says a crying woman, "Justice for all. What is the justice for the poor people?" With this central question of the film, the camera pulls back and upward again, showing the expanse of torn, brown soil. The final moment of the film is another aerial shot, showing the lot still empty, still brown, devoid of plant and human life. "As of June 2008," reads a final title card, "two years after the eviction, Mr. Horowitz has built nothing on the site." Then the film cuts to black and rolls the closing credits.

The Garden thus ends with the community defeated and with its hopes to save the garden disappointed. Even as Horowitz is in his right, legally, the film's strong viewer alignment with the farmers creates a deep sense of injustice. Kennedy has freely admitted that his film is told "from the point of view of the farmers" (Poland 2010) but insists that he gave everyone involved in the conflict a chance to speak on camera.[15] These efforts notwithstanding, some reviewers have been critical of the film's biases. Catsoulis writes that Kennedy's "focus on

---

[15] According to Kennedy, this includes Horowitz, who first agreed to an interview and then cancelled, forcing the filmmaker to portray his side of the story "through interviews that he did" with other people "and the public record of his disposition" (Poland 2010).

individual farmers leaves many questions unanswered" (2009). Adam Keleman complains that "the city and real estate developers are not given much attention compared to the clearly suffering, bulldozed farm workers" and calls *The Garden* "a one-sided portrait," while admitting that "the documentary digs deep into the racial and monetary problems of a tumultuous, melting-pot community" (2009). Kennedy, however, has defended his creative choices:

> I didn't want to make it a sociological study . . . . I wanted it to be from the point of view of the characters living it, and we have to try and figure out . . . through their faces, through their words, through the hard evidence, what is right and what is wrong. I find that much more engaging . . . . That goes to the root of what kind of documentaries you want to make (Poland interview 2010)

It is viewers' engagement in the farmer's struggle for food justice that Kennedy values the most, and he deliberately foregrounds the words of those who are too often dismissed or ignored. *The Garden* "speaks *with* the South Central Farmers to address a host of issues surrounding local politics, citizenship, racism, food production, agrarian myths, neoliberalism, and more," observes Enck-Wanzer, and it thereby creates a cinematic stage for the farmer-activists on which to "enact a geo-body politics of knowledge that is consistently subverted, even by supporters, vis-a-vis modern-colonial rationality" (2011, 363). It is in this context that Kennedy wants his film to pose a larger question: "Are we, all of us as citizens, trying to live by the fact that justice for all is something we want to fight for . . . or is it just a pipe dream that we bring up to use as a slogan now and again?" (Poland interview 2010). Ultimately, *The Garden* asks viewers to interrogate their own implication in the structures that endanger the existence of community gardens like the South Central Farm and to ensure that their actions are aligned with their moral stance of food justice.

With some viewers, this strategy seems to have succeeded. "*The Garden* is a gripping and enraging film," writes Naomi Starkman, emphasizing the emotional dimensions of her own moral response to it. That they include rage might be seen as problematic, but philosophers have defended anger as "the emotion of injustice" (Baily 2018, 93) and argued that it is "a morally necessary response to wrongdoing" (Thomason 2020, 83). Sue Kim makes a related point in *On Anger: Race, Cognition, Narrative* (2014, 2), stating that "anger also reflects conflicts within a society." These views all emphasize the moral and political value of the emotion. Moreover, empathic anger, as viewers are likely to feel on behalf of characters, can be a strong motivator for prosocial action (Hofman 2000).[16]

---

[16] In an article surveying empirical research on empathic anger, Bringle, Hedgepath, and Wall conclude that it should be promoted "as a basis for action directed at social justice issues" (2018, 1).

Starkman seems to be aware of this, given how she concludes her review of *The Garden*: "Go see the film and learn how you can support local urban farms" (2009). This immediate link between viewing and *acting* is precisely what impact-oriented films are invested in and what film scholar Dirk Eitzen has called the documentary form's "peculiar appeal" (2005, 183).[17] Eitzen argues that the documentary form makes moral "entreaties" to viewers by the very nature of its nonfictionality, which inevitably reminds them that what they see on the screen has repercussions in the real world that they might act upon (183). Feeling moral outrage at the end of *The Garden* thus might lead to the conclusion Starkman suggests – even as the South Central Farm is lost, there are other community garden projects ongoing, perhaps in viewers' immediate neighborhoods, that need their support. In a slightly different way, such an appeal has also been made by the second film I want to consider here, Todd Darling's *Occupy the Farm*, which chronicles the struggle over another urban agriculture project – the Gill Tract Farm in Albany, CA – but ultimately presents a more hopeful vision.

Food Justice as Utopian Social Action: Todd Darling's *Occupy the Farm*

The Gill Tract Farm belongs to UC Berkeley and thus to a land-grant university, designated by the State of California to receive the benefits of the Morrill Acts of 1862 and 1890, which "provided each state with 'public' lands to sell in order to raise funds to establish universities" (Joseph A. Myers Center 2021). Lauded as the first major federal funding for public education, the Morrill Acts had dire consequences for California Indians who lost 150,000 acres of Indigenous land that funded the University of California. This not only ties UC Berkeley to a long history of Native dispossession, but its founding as a land-grant institution also requires it to do agricultural research beneficial to the public. However, the portion of the Gill Tract dedicated to agricultural research has been shrinking over time, from 104 acres in 1928 down to only 14 acres – the same size as the South Central Farm. In 2012, UC Berkeley planned to sell even more of its land to corporate developers. What it had not considered was that such plans would come to the attention of the Occupy movement, which, a few months earlier, had protested the university's fee hike by occupying one of its buildings. On Earth Day 2012, two hundred Occupy activists snapped the padlock to the Gill Tract Farm and trespassed to plant 15,000 seedlings on two acres of that land within just two days. It was

---

[17] Impact-oriented filmmaking has been understood as a mode of filmmaking that deliberately seeks to "harness the power of storytelling to inspire change, raise awareness and promote sustainable development" (Aksu 2023).

also the day on which filming began for Todd Darling's *Occupy the Farm*. As was the case for Kennedy and *The Garden*, Darling had not planned to make this documentary. He happened to be in the area to make another film about urban community gardens in Oakland when he heard about the occupation. And like Kennedy, Darling started filming *in medias res*, catching up on the backstory as he was documenting Occupy's direct action and the responses by UC Berkeley's administration, faculty, and police force on the one hand, and the local community on the other.[18]

The Occupy movement came to prominence in September 2011, when a group of left-wing activists assembled in Zuccotti Park in the Financial District of Lower Manhattan to protest economic inequality and the influence of money in politics. Occupy the Farm was one of the more successful direct actions of this diverse movement, which has been both lauded for its collective identity and criticized for its lack of direction (Kavada 2015; Roman-Alcalá 2017). The group's justification for occupying the Gill Tract was that the university's plans to sell the land for development were in violation of its charter and that the plant genetics research currently done on part of the land was only benefiting corporate interests and the university itself. By contrast, planting 15,000 seedlings on two acres and opening the doors to the public would bring fresh food to low-income communities in Albany as well as nearby Richmond and Oakland. As Rebecca Tarlau notes, the occupation "was not spontaneous; it took months of planning that ranged from organizing community support for the action to growing over 15,000 starter plants that could be planted on the land" (2012). Moreover, the chosen starting date, April 22, was meant to show solidarity with *La Via Campesina*, thus relating the action to a much larger story about agricultural appropriation, exploitation, and the struggle for food sovereignty.

In Darling's film, that connection is apparent from the first minute. Unlike Kennedy, he chooses to open his story with footage from the day of the farmers' eviction, thus giving away the (apparent) ending. The sequence intercuts coverage from several news stations with original footage shot inside the Occupy camp on the Gill Tract. A policeman informs reporters about the potential use of force, including chemical agents, as activists leave the premises, trays of plants in their hands. Over these images, we hear the calm voice of one of the Occupy farmers, Ashoka Finley. "There's no individual that can take credit for what happened." The phrase at once deflects responsibility and stresses the importance of community. As the opening credits appear, Finley looks into the camera

---

[18] Darling explained in an interview that he relied on other filmmakers providing material. The footage from the first day of the occupation included in the film was shot by Peter Menchini (Myers 2021).

and adds: "Twenty-six million people, just under ten percent of the U.S. population doesn't have access to fresh food." He thus links the occupation to the country's larger problem of food injustice and apartheid, and the next shot shows a Black woman driving through Richmond counting liquor stores – and not a single grocery store. "It is really more an issue of food distribution than of scarcity," comments a scientist. None of these people are named at this point, but all standing on this side of the food justice struggle have been presented.

As in *The Garden*, the protagonists of *Occupy the Farm* are a group of farmer-activists who fight to defend an urban community garden against the destructive force of capitalist interests. Unlike in the case of the South Central Farm, however, these farmers have only very recently established themselves on the ground, without invitation. Moreover, they are experienced in Occupy's direct action tactics – activists turned farmers rather than the other way around. Aside from Finley, who is one of the leading figures of Occupy the Farm and a political economy graduate of UC Berkeley, they include two other recent UC Berkeley graduates with farming backgrounds, Anya Kamenskaya and Effie Rawlings, as well as Gopal Dayaneni, a seasoned community organizer who attended UC Berkley as an undergraduate. Given that the ostentatious antagonist in this struggle over the Gill Tract Farm is UC Berkeley, the fact that all four main protagonists have ties to the school is relevant, as is their privileged social standing. However, as Finley noted during a discussion at UC Santa Barbara's Carsey-Wolf Center in 2015: "My standing won't matter if I don't *do* something about these situations right now." This need for *agency* and *action* is at the center of the film and the reason why Finley joined the Occupy movement with the initial goal to occupy a university building to protest the student fee hikes following the financial crisis in 2008. As he explains in the film, he was stunned by the students' inertia: "They had this emotional response, but the emotional response didn't inspire action. And so, I think what's really kind of crucial in this moment is [to] create outlets for that emotive response . . . and allow them to express that in a way that creates something larger than themselves." The Occupy the Farm movement was meant to function as such an outlet and larger creation, animated by hope and action rather than wishful thinking. The film spells out the group's goals in large white letters: (1) SAVE THE FARM FROM BECOMING A REAL-ESTATE DEVELOPMENT and (2) KEEP THE LAND FOR AGRICULTURAL USE AND EDUCATION. Surrendering narrative agency in part to the activists, it gives them the platform of a feature documentary to voice their demands.

Like the protagonists of *The Garden*, the Occupy farmers have some prominent supporters. Rather than actors and musicians, however, they are tenured academics at UC Berkeley such as Jeff Romm, a professor in the Department of Environmental Science, Policy & Management, and Miguel Altieri, a professor of Agro-Ecology. The surrounding community in Albany has also responded positively to the direct action, with people visiting and some of them joining the farmers. On the other side of the conflict stand UC Berkeley administrators, among them Vice Chancellor Edward Denton and Keith Gilless, Dean of the College of Natural Resources and directly responsible for the Gill Tract. Because it is up against former students supported by tenured faculty and community members – and because it is still stunned by the negative press coverage of its poor handling of the previous Occupy action – the university is careful in its dealing with the occupation. Its representatives show understanding, even sympathy, for the cause of the activists while insisting that they cannot condone their approach. Dan Mogulof, Executive Director for Public Affairs, adds that he is "not sure if what they're doing can be fairly or accurately described as civil disobedience" since the activists are trespassing on UC land. The fact that the activists have not yet been removed from the Gill Tract is framed as a sign of the university's generosity, calm, and patience, as is its willingness to meet with the activists to discuss their demands. Yet regardless of these gestures, the situation is getting increasingly more difficult for the Occupy farmers as UC police lock the entrance, declaring that "persons entering or remaining on the Gill Tract are subject to arrest and prosecution," and the university cuts off their water supply. This decision makes for moving images of community support as people from the surrounding neighborhoods haul containers of water to the fence and help the farmers inside keep their seedlings alive. One of the Occupy activists calls it "the best thing … for cooperative learning because now everybody who has come through here has had the experience of carrying water like an average world citizen – something most of us have never even come close to thinking about doing in a day." Creating that "relationship between our labor, our water, our community, our food, our education system," she suggests, is a valuable lesson for the farmer-activists and their supporters alike.

As a result of this outpour of community support, the university changes strategies, now arguing that ending the occupation of the Gill Tract is an "issue of standing up and protecting academic freedom" with reference to Damon Lisch, a maize genetics biologist who is unable to carry out his grant-funded research work there. Arguments by supporters like Altieri, who seek to show that "the coexistence between research and the occupiers is possible," are going unheard; the activists' strategic decision to remove the camp infrastructure also does not make a difference. On Day 22 of the occupation, UC police show up outside the fence in riot gear in the name of academic freedom. The camera shows the stunned faces of the defeated farmer-activists as they get arrested or grudgingly leave the tract, but there is none of the existential anguish pervading *The Garden*'s brutal eviction scene. Just as important, in terms of imagery, there are no bulldozers destroying a veritable garden filled with mature crops and fruit trees. On the contrary, a moment of visual humor shows one of the activists jumping the fence to water the seedlings as a jeering crowd eggs him on and UC policemen are chasing him in a golf cart. The seedlings remain in the ground, and, six weeks later, the Occupy activists trespass again to harvest. Their greatest victory, however, is that the eviction creates so much controversy that one of the prospective corporate tenants, Whole Foods, terminates its lease with the developers, endangering the real-estate deal. In the ensuing negotiations, the activists manage to secure 1.3 acres of the Gill Tract for a community farm.

Occupy the Farm thus ends on a happy, even triumphant note, but as Ernest Hardy has observed, it is "almost impossible to come away from the film feeling anything but unease" as it "illustrates the staggering extent to which corporate interests dictate policy and shape scientific research" (2014). That is the historical truth that Hardy calls "the grim dark cloud hovering over this Occupy victory lap" (2014). Darling appears to have been well aware of that cloud, but he was very much invested in keeping the outlook of his film hopeful. Asked whether he is a filmmaker or an activist, he responded that he sees himself as an observer who felt "the responsibility to tell [the story] accurately and as completely as possible in a dynamic way" (2015). However, he also admitted that

> the feeling of being in sync with the people and the story was unusual . . . . To see this kind of . . . hyper-local activism, this hyper-local active resistance and creativity in the same place doing something so obviously good was like 'wow!' This is something that anyone can do in a 15-minute bike ride from their house. There is some stressed public resource, there is something that people can use their own personal leverage and their own friends and do something that is of great consequence, and it can multiply. (2015)

There is an emphasis on the active components of hope in this answer: the positive expectation, the agency to make it happen, and the trust that it is possible. However, even as he acknowledges his own views being "in sync" with those of the Occupy farmers, Darling insists he is not an activist. Like Kennedy, he sees his job as filmmaker to offer an accurate understanding of what is at stake in a way that is engaging. His emphasis on transferability echoes Starkman's review of *The Garden*, implying that what transpires on the screen should serve as an inspiration to become active in one's own community.

Jeannette Catsoulis did not see it the same way. As in her review of *The Garden*, she uses irony to belittle Darling's efforts in the *New York Times*, stating that he "is so busy fist-pumping for urban farming – and so dazzled by his granola heroes – that naysayers must be demeaned and denigrated" (2014). Reading Catsoulis's reviews of the two films, written five years apart, is striking not only because of their similar titles, but also because she appears to be deeply appalled by the directors' perceived *bias* in favor of those fighting for food justice. "Sun-dappled interviews with beaming amateur farmers lay out the benefits of locally grown veggies," she complains in her review of *Occupy the Farm*, "but their opponents are not so prettily lighted or ideologically indulged." Denigrative tone aside, Catsoulis's reaction appears to reveal a bias against engaged and impact-oriented filmmaking along with a belief that documentaries should be "objective" in the treatment of their subject matter, giving equal screen time and narrative agency to all parties in a conflict. This may be a limiting belief since, as Mathew Abbot puts it, "being objective does not mean taking a purely dispassionate stance toward one's subjects but treating them without prejudice or moralism and letting them reveal themselves" (2019, 108).[19] Moreover, as Helen Hughes has shown, the makers of "green" documentaries are often "not only engaged but involved" (2014, 5). Catsoulis's indignation thus also points beyond the two films to the larger issue they are dealing with. As Darling has put it: "If you go down any path in the food movement, you end up at some problem of justice" (Discussion Carsey-Wolf Center 2015) and faced with a problem of (in)justice and inequity, the question is whether filmmakers should indeed be impartial regardless of what is at stake. It is, after all, one of the affordances of documentary film that it can extend narrative agency to people who have been silenced, ignored, or disregarded. This may be truer for the Latinx working-class protagonists of *The Garden* than it is for the college-educated "granola heroes" of *Occupy the Farm*, but in a society shaped by the values of neoliberal capitalism, the voices of all food justice activists might need some amplification.

Conclusion

Documentaries such as *The Garden* and *Occupy the Farm*, which frame individual acts of community resistance to the neoliberal appropriation of public space within a larger moral argument about food (in)justice, cannot help but present only a slice of historical reality. Kennedy and Darling both shot much of their footage while the respective conflicts were unfolding, their direct access and personal proximity to the protagonists giving their documentaries a sense of

---

[19] Bill Nichols argues that when watching a documentary, we understand that it "will stand back from being a pure document or transcription of these events to a make a comment on them, or to offer a perspective on them" (2001, 38).

immediacy and urgency. Yet, at some point, filming had to stop and the material had to be edited and released. History, meanwhile, continued.

The final minutes of *The Garden* show the South Central Farmers regrouping after the eviction, some of them continuing to farm on seven acres in South Los Angeles offered by the city, others on eighty acres in Bakersfield, California. It is a sad conclusion to the narrative arc of the film but some of the farmers were not done fighting, making multiple attempts to appeal to the court decision, all of them unsuccessful. In 2017, when Los Angeles passed its version of the Urban Agriculture Incentive Zones Act and Horowitz's tract, eleven years after the eviction, was still lying fallow, the "South Central Farm Restoration Committee" tried one more time to revive the garden with a petition and yet another legal effort (Kuipers 2020). Two years later, the farmers' final challenge ended with a 12–0 vote against them by the Los Angeles City Council (Reyes 2019). The fourteen-acre lot at East 41st and South Alameda Streets is now home to two warehouses, blending in with the surrounding landscape of asphalt and concrete. Even though it was more successful by comparison, the fight over the Gill Tract was also far from over after filming for *Occupy the Farm* concluded. At the time of my writing, the UC Gill Tract Community Farm still thrives on 1.3 acres, conducting "collaborative community-driven research, education, and extension focused on ecological farming and food justice," and fostering "equitable economies, a healthy environment, and increased resilience in vulnerable communities." However, there is now also a Sprouts supermarket on part of the land, and the university's ten-year agreement ended in 2023. Even more important, the Sogorea Te Land Trust got involved with the project after reminding everyone that the Gill Tract sits on unceded Lisjan Ohlone land. Community gardens are often located in contested spaces, remind us Mares and Peña, "in this sense, urban gardens and farms are often a communal expression of a community's political power" (2010, 265), which includes the power to tell one's story and get heard.

The question of narrative agency can indeed be a difficult one for engaged filmmakers who want to elevate the voices of those who have less political power. Not only do they risk accusations of bias, but there is also the question of representation and appropriation. Kennedy and Darling are both white and outsiders to the communities they represent in their films. As I have previously argued, an outsider perspective on issues of justice must not necessarily be useless or inherently problematic; it even can have advantages. Moreover as we have seen, the documentary mode allows for the partial surrender of narrative agency to the protagonists and a more dialogic process of creation and representation. However, this approach comes with its own set of limitations that have been viewed in an increasingly critical light in recent years. I will explore some of the ways in which filmmakers and food justice activists have grappled with the problem of representation in the next chapter, turning my attention to narratives of defiant gardening in Black communities in Detroit, Carlston, and Albany, which project radical hope and resilience but also remind us of the continued fragility of community gardens in contested urban spaces.

2 Projecting Resilience

In Mark MacInnis's 2009 documentary film *Urban Roots*, Malik Kenyatta Yakini stands in the green expanse of the seven-acre D-Town Farm in Detroit and talks about the difficulties of getting young people interested in community gardening: "Typically, when teenagers come out [here], one of the first things that comes out of their mouths is 'I thought slavery was over.'" As the co-founder and Executive Director of the Detroit Black Community Food Security Network (DBCFSN) that operates the D-Town Farm, Yakini sees a need to reframe Black agricultural work as an active and hopeful way of building food sovereignty and community resilience by teaching "self-determination. We're not waiting on anybody to give us a grant," he explains in the film to a group of Black youth, "this is something we see a need for and so we're making it happen." In Yakini's view, a crucial element of teaching self-determination is a reconnection to African ancestral knowledge and the fact that "Black people's relationship to the land did not start or end with enslavement." Nineteenth-century educators such as Booker T. Washington and his director of agriculture at Tuskegee Institute, George Washington Carver, already tried to establish such reconnections to leave behind "the vicious circles of peonage and sharecropping" (Klestil 2023, 228). Community garden projects run by Black Americans go at least as far back as 1967, when the activist Fannie Lou Hamer purchased forty acres of land in the Mississippi Delta, launching the Freedom Farms Cooperative to empower poor Black farmers and sharecroppers.[20] However, despite such efforts, the long history of exploitation continues to alienate Black Americans from agricultural work. In her book *Farming While Black* (2018, 3) Leah Penniman remembers that the only consistent story she was told growing up "about Black people and the land was about slavery and sharecropping, about coercion and brutality and misery and sorrow". Combined with the large-scale loss of Black-owned land over the twentieth century (Francis et al. 2022), many Black Americans have lost touch with their agricultural traditions. One way to recover them has been through community farming projects such as

---

[20] The acreage itself was a comment on General William T. Sherman's notoriously unfulfilled promise during the American Civil War that plots of land no larger than forty acres would be allotted to freed Black families.

D-Town Farm and Penniman's own Soul Fire Farm, which I will consider later in this chapter.

Such gardening and farming projects, I will argue, follow all four of the pathways toward radical hope that have been outlined by Mosley et al. (2020): They educate their communities about the history of oppression along with the actions of resistance taken to transform these conditions; they embrace ancestral pride; they envision equitable possibilities; and they create meaning and purpose in life by adopting an orientation to social and environmental justice. From such radically hopeful endeavors, it is but a small step toward utopian thinking. "If utopia arises from desire," writes Ruth Levitas, "the transformation of reality and the realisation of utopia depend upon hope, upon not only wishful thinking but will-full action" (1990, 199). This focus on practicability and transformative action is also at the heart of Eric Olen Wright's concept of "real utopias." The challenge of envisioning them, explains Wright, "is to elaborate clear-headed, rigorous, and viable alternatives to existing social institutions that both embody our deepest aspirations for human flourishing and take seriously the problem of practical design" (2007, 37). In this understanding, real utopias capture the spirit of social dreaming, but they are focused on "what it takes to bring those aspirations to life" (37). It is in this sense that the narratives of food justice I consider here are cautiously utopian. They have their eyes on the as-of-yet unrealized possibilities of the future while staying rooted in the messy struggle necessary to work toward them.

With *Urban Roots*, the first part of this chapter turns to a film that represents the diverse community of farmers that has grown in and out of postindustrial Detroit. Robert Emmett notes that MacInnis is one of several recent filmmakers who examine "the scope of community gardening as a movement of resistance to local political corruption and the monopolizing tendencies of neoliberalism" (2016, 134). I would also include Scott Hamilton Kennedy and Todd Darling in this group, but what makes *Urban Roots* different from their films is that it chronicles the relative success of a diverse web of community farms rather than the embittered struggle over one, and that it showcases how grassroots-led gardening programs aim to reconnect Black people with their African cultural roots. As in the previous chapter, I am interested in the distribution of narrative agency in the depiction of such projects as well as in the filmmaker's relationship to it and the cinematic means by which it is conveyed. I will argue that *Urban Roots* manages to be an ultimately hopeful film because of when and where it was filmed and because MacInnis emphasizes the multifaceted benefits of urban community farming over the greater neoliberal forces circumscribing it.

The second part of the chapter considers two other resilient Black community farming projects – the Fresh Future Farm in North Charleston, South Carolina, and the Soul Fire Farm outside Albany, New York – through the lenses of two documentary films and a range of digital media channels. Focusing on the material efforts and narrative agency of the two Black farmers who started these garden projects, Germaine Jenkins and Leah Penniman, it explores how they work to build *community resilience* as a way "to adjust, withstand, and absorb disturbance, and to reorganize while undergoing change." This working definition of resilience, proposed by sociologist Monica White (2018), "emphasizes structural approaches and community engagement, including types of indigenous knowledge, emotional experiences, and intra/interracial exchanges that communities need in order to adapt to unforeseen conditions." It will inform my analysis of the manifold ways in which Jenkins, Penniman, and other Black farmers have harnessed material, political, and narrative agency to engage their own communities as well as larger audiences in their narratives about the need for food justice and the ways they hope to bring it about.

Stories of Decline and Resilience in Detroit: Mark MacInnis's *Urban Roots*

Urban Roots opens with upbeat piano music and a series of black-and-white shots from Detroit's illustrious past. Grainy archival footage showing the early days of assembly-line automobile production is intercut with nostalgic black title cards that inform viewers that "Mr. Ford's Model T made Detroit the automotive capital of the world" and that "enterprising workers came to this industrial powerhouse in search of the American Dream." The next shot shows suburbs of Detroit in the 1950s filled with elegantly dressed Black couples and their children playing on tree-lined sidewalks next to groomed front yards and neat houses. "Detroit was a true melting pot at the forefront of commerce and culture," says the next title card, a city that "with a daring imagination and a spirit of progress ... led the nation towards a better tomorrow." Black-and-white footage showing downtown Detroit during the height of the city's prosperity is followed by a cut to black and an abrupt change in music, pace, and imagery. Then, rendered in stark colors and accompanied by melancholic Motown music, a slow flow of static shots documents Detroit's collapse: industrial wastelands, rotting houses, broken infrastructure, heaps of trash and debris, overgrown by vegetation. Some shots show what is left of the city's inhabitants, all of them Black. "The people that lived on this block had no idea that this was gonna happen," says an off-screen voice as a long tracking shot shows more broken houses. "We worked in the factories, we partied, we had good times, we raised families, we went to school. We just couldn't imagine someone saying: 'This closed down, let's move out.'" The sense of hope and opportunity that opened the sequence gives way to disbelief and devastation.

As is now known around the world, this dramatic decline *did* happen to Detroit in the span of just a few decades. In a 2011 article on urban gardening as a mode of Black resistance that builds on her extensive sociological research, Monica White explains that the "transformations of the automobile industry, along with the subsequent shrinking of the working and middle classes, have left Detroiters mired in poverty-induced challenges, including reduced city services, poor-quality education, high rates of unemployment, crime, housing foreclosures, and little or no access to healthy food" (14). According to the U.S. Census, between 1950 and 2020, Detroit lost two-thirds of its population, from 1.8 million down to 639,111, with about 77 percent of those left behind identifying as Black. Because of this population loss, the city has over 40,000 vacant lots and the entire inner city was declared a food desert in 2010 after most of the supermarket chains had pulled out. More than any other American city, Detroit has become the symbol of postindustrial decay. "Every American should visit Detroit," says urban designer Alex Krieger in MacInnis's film, "just to kind of experience how much abuse we bring to urbanization sometimes . . . and to be aware of the fact that cities don't always just grow in perpetuity; there are periods where in fact they decline and therefore other options [that] might reemerge during that decline need to be considered." One of those options is urban agriculture, including larger profit-oriented farms, backyard subsistence farming, urban community gardens, and mixed formats that straddle the boundaries between profit and nonprofit.

Detroit's vibrant and diverse farming scene has attracted media interest as well as the scientific community in recent years, and it has given the city's overarching declension narrative a curiously hopeful, even cautiously utopian bend (Colasanti et al. 2012; Pothukuchi 2015). White, who was still a PhD student when MacInnis interviewed her for his film, sums up her insights from speaking to Black farmers as follows: "There is all kinds of different sort of side effects of what happens when people garden – crime rates reduce, property values increase – but . . . I recognized that Black farmers were really interested in engaging in urban agriculture as a way of having some control over their existence, over the food system." This claim to agency and food sovereignty is foregrounded throughout *Urban Roots*. Compared to the more plot-driven dramas I discussed in the first chapter, MacInnis's film has a slower pace, more contemplative and much looser in structure. Through archival footage, graphics, and an impressive number of interviews set amidst thriving crops, the film tells a patchwork story about people who are not only transforming abandoned lots into small-scale urban farms but have their minds set on creating a future in which most or all the fresh produce needed in Detroit is grown within city limits.

As MacInnis visits the farms, it is the people who work on them who do all the talking. Time and again, they relate the same experiences and goals: the need for local food in the absence of grocery stores and the visceral joy they feel growing and eating it; the pride in their achievements and the fact that they are using (mostly uncertified) organic growing practices; the desire for self-determination; the joy of engaging children in the farm work; the ability to give back to the community and lift people out of poverty by enabling them to grow and sell their own food. Food security. Food sovereignty. Food justice. These are the recurring themes even as the farms have different origin stories, from a wish to find out whether one can make a living growing food on five "adopted lots," which grew into the Brother Nature Farm, to the 1.25 acres of Earthworks, a program of the Capuchin Soup Kitchen, which grows its vegetables predominantly for use in a soup kitchen that gives out 600 meals a day. Elmhurst is a treatment facility for alcohol and drug abuse that keeps a public garden in a nearby vacant lot as a way for patients to work off their community service hours. D-Town Farm is operated by the DBCFSN and is deeply invested in its educational and youth programs. The Field of Our Dreams Mobile Market, owned by two Black farmers, drives around town to sell fresh food and vegetables to whoever needs them. The diversity of the farmers portrayed in the film is striking, not only in terms of race, but also when it comes to gender, education, class, and age. "We have people who are educators," says Malik Yakini about the community on the D-Town Farm, "we have people who are factory workers, we have people who are unemployed. We have a wide variety of people of all walks of life, but the thing is they all see the necessity for us to come together to create a greater degree of self-reliance." This is representative of how the embodied practice of gardening can work across divides.[21] In *Freedom Farmers* (2018), White argues that grassroots community projects such as the ones growing in Detroit are a form of "everyday resistance" that is "enacted by individuals or small groups" who are not only growing food together, but also "building knowledge, skills, community, and economic independence" (6) as well as "collective agency" (7). It is thus appropriate that *Urban Roots* gives the farmers what we might call *collective narrative agency* by presenting an interwoven chorus of voices that speak for themselves.

Like Kennedy and Darling, MacInnis is an outsider to the community he portrays, and he has emphasized that it was the farmers who inspired him to

---

[21] As Emmett notes, any account of the American environmental justice movement "ought to be supplemented by recognizing the significant achievements made by coalitions that cross, class, gender, and racial divisions, such as the community garden movement" (2016, 139). On this point, see also Alkon and Norgaard (2009).

make this film and that their voices and visions shaped it (*Imbibe & Inspire* 2012). The result is a radically hopeful narrative set in what Greg Willerer of Brother Nature Farm calls "a space of possibilities" – a term that resonates with Eric Olen Wright's "real utopias" and the challenge of elaborating "clear-headed, rigorous, and viable alternatives to existing social institutions that . . . take seriously the problem of practical design" (2007, 37). A good example is the Earthworks Urban Farm, introduced by farmer Patrick Crouch with an allusion to Tim Burton's *Charlie and the Chocolate Factory* (1971) and the moment when Willy Wonka opens the door to all the delicacies waiting behind it. Accompanied by the song "Pure Imagination," the sequence intercuts creamy wide-angle shots of the farm with colorful closeups of the harvested vegetables and their preparation in the Capuchin Soup Kitchen. However, the nonprofit is also invested in societal transformation. "We are really focused on this concept of food justice," explains Crouch as he presents the farm's transplant distribution concept, which involves growing over 100,000 transplants and distributing them to gardeners all over Detroit. "By the small effort of us growing the transplants, we are facilitating others the opportunity to grow their own food. This is making significant impacts into people's capacity to provide for themselves . . . and hopefully also providing them with some income .. that's really where we see the future going." The film presents Keith Love's Field of our Dreams Mobile Market as a practical application of the concept, demonstrating how it brings a steady income and self-esteem for the former drug addict and fresh local vegetables for the community. "When everything collapses," reads the blurb for *Urban Roots*, "plant your field of dreams." Love and the other Detroit farmers portrayed in the film have done exactly that.

However, regardless of how radically hopeful these farming projects look in the film, they are affected by the inherent fragility of all urban agriculture. "You don't need a title or a deed," sings the musician and urban farmer Tommy Spaghetti at the beginning of *Urban Roots*, "you can plant a garden, nobody cares." That has been true for many years, and yet one of the potential future antagonists of the farmers is the City of Detroit, which, as former mayor Dennis Archer points out, "reserves the right to take the land back" if new opportunities for creating revenue ensue because it is not zoned for agriculture. The film also pays attention to two related developments that might pose a threat to the city's grassroots farming community: increased gentrification due to the "beautification effect" and countercultural vibe of the farms and gardens, which, in combination with cheap rents attract young people from all over the country. City planner Kathryn Underwood suggests that the city does not have "a pulse of . . . . how many young people are coming into the city . . . to do something different, to do eco-villages and try new kinds of living." However, a 2022 study found no direct association between urban gardens and gentrification in Detroit and cautioned that "racialized narratives around gardens and redevelopment risk undermining long-standing connections between Detroit's gardens and environmental justice (Hawes, Gounaridis & Newell)."[22] The other and perhaps more immediate threat comes from large-scale commercial farming operations, such as Hantz Farms. In the film, the farm's vice president Matt Allen points to abandoned lots as he proposes his own utopian vision of building the largest commercial urban farm in the U.S. on 5000 acres of "blighted" land and lists aesthetic and economic benefits for the city and the community. The smaller grassroot farmers, however, note that Hantz is not organic and that their plan will at best create some minimum-wage jobs. "He doesn't have a clue of what it takes to get this land ready, that's the joke," comments Andrew Kemp with barely suppressed contempt, referring to the large amounts of concrete and contaminants often buried in urban lots.[23] Another farmer, Nefer Ra Barber, states that Hantz simply "doesn't understand community, it's basically bottom-line dollars" – a reminder that one person's utopia can be many others' dystopia and that all modes of urban agriculture are not the same.

Here, too, it is instructive to continue following the story after *Urban Roots* was wrapped up and released in 2009. Only one year later, Detroit legalized many urban farming endeavors with large-scale rezoning of its inner city (Paddeu 2017). It is tempting to see this as good news, mutually beneficial for urban farmers and the shrinking city. However, Hantz Farms ballooned into something of a local supervillain when, in 2012, John Hantz promised the city $30 million of his own money to clean up not 5,000 but 10,000 acres in one of the most devastated neighborhoods in Detroit, now determined to create largest urban *tree farm* in the U.S. It may not come as a surprise to those who have seen *Urban Roots* that Hantz has since met with a lot of resistance from residents and other farmers, enough to inspire another documentary, Sean King O'Grady's *Land Grab* (2016). Malik Yakini – who also appears in this second film – explains that the community is "concerned about large amounts of land being amassed by wealthy white men." Hantz, who is allowed to speak at length in O'Grady's film, frames his purchases as an altruistic beautifying operation, whereas other residents accuse the city of using the new zoning code to give the mogul preferred treatment and better rates than everyone else, making it difficult to compete (Brooker 2023). To date, Hantz Farms has turned about 140 acres of "blighted" land into brown lots filled with seedlings that they promise will become woodlands. Moreover, Hantz fueled concerns about speculation

---

[22] On other narratives representing the threat of gentrification for urban gardens, see Sulimma (2023).

[23] On overlooked toxins in urban community gardens, see Malone (2022).

when he sold off $2.8 million in properties in 2021 as interest started to grow in Detroit neighborhoods (Pinho 2021). Even more remarkable, then, is that *Land Grab* ultimately concludes that Hantz's actions do not constitute a land grab. Given that a trailer for the film is featured on the Hantz Farms website, one might wonder once again about narrative agency in relation to food justice and the forces of capitalism.

What makes urban farming projects fragile even in a postindustrial space such as Detroit is the fact that most of the farmers do not own the land they grow on. They may have "adopted" a few abandoned lots without official permission, or they may have leased it for an amount that allows their work to be profitable. But even as the land is getting rezoned and farming thus becomes legal, many of them do not have the funds to buy it or they face bureaucratic obstacles tied to their class status and/or ethnic identity. "Institutionalized racism," observes Mark Bittman, has "made Black Americans – whose presence in the United States was as long-term and legitimate as that of any other except for Indigenous people – the most landless group in the country" (2022, 271). Black landownership sharply declined over the twentieth century: whereas in 1910 about 14 percent of U.S. farmers were Black, owning more than 16 million acres of land, the latest Census of Agriculture shows only 1 percent of farmers to be Black, owning less than 5 million acres, which amounts to a loss of roughly $326 billion worth of acreage (Francis et al. 2022). Given the general fragility of urban agriculture, the issue of landownership thus emerges as a crucial factor in tackling structural inequalities, ecological sustainability, and community development. Black farmers such as Germaine Jenkins and Leah Penniman, to whom I will now turn, have been trying to address these issues both in the agricultural community projects they have founded and in the way they claim narrative agency to share their utopian visions of a more equitable future.[24]

Taking Charge: Bridget Besaw's *Rooted* and Penniman's *Farming While Black*

Labeling itself a "documentary film about food apartheid in America,' the trailer for Bridget Besaw's *Rooted* opens with archival footage showing First Lady Michelle Obama as she declares that "23.5 million Americans, including 6.5 million children" live in food deserts. Cut to a medium shot of food justice activist Germaine Jenkins standing amid the crops she is growing on her Fresh Future Farm in North Charleston, South Carolina. "It is expensive as hell to be poor in the United States," Jenkins says into the camera, which is why, a few

---

[24] For a recent documentary about Black landownership, see Eternal Polk's *Gaining Ground* (2023).

years ago, she "went to the city and told them that we were gonna take a vacant lot, turn it into a farm, create jobs and beautiful produce at the same time, and a grocery store in a place where there hasn't been one in over eleven years before we started." The trailer also features civil rights activist Millicent Brown and Black Lives Matter co-founder Hawk Newsome, who claims that "this food injustice fight is more important than the Black Lives Matter movement" because "we have more control over this food injustice fight than we have over anything else that we face." Firmly established by these testimonies as someone who belongs to the "civil rights workers and warriors of their generation," Jenkins uses the term *food apartheid* to emphasize the structural issues behind the injustice that people in low-income communities often do not have adequate access to fresh food to stay healthy: "Researchers can tell you your life expectancy based on your zip code." The Fresh Futures Farm is meant to alleviate this injustice and the trailer mentions that the lease for the lot on which Jenkins established the farm will be up "in September 2019" and might not get renewed. "If I wasn't a Black woman," Jenkins says, "the level of disrespect I'm asked to tolerate would not happen." Although she is battling health problems, she is committed to keeping her farm, and the film is supposed to help her garner broad support. It is thus one more project to remind us of the fragility of urban agriculture; yet, in this case, the state of uncertainty extends to the question of narrative agency.

September 2019 has long passed, and the Fresh Futures Farm is still around. The updated release date currently given for *Rooted* on the film's website is 2024, and it is scheduled to premiere at the New Orleans Film Festival. In two connected (and now deleted) statements, posted on June 16, 2020, Besaw and Jenkins explained why they decided to put it on hold. "Years into the project," wrote Besaw, we find ourselves in this pivotal moment, reflecting deeply on privilege and who should be telling which stories. Filmmaking is a deeply collaborative process, and to that end, I will redouble my efforts to bring more Black storytellers into the process." Jenkins, in her statement, wrote that "this new direction is bittersweet because [Besaw's] cinematography and storytelling skills jump off the screen in a powerful way .... However, as a Black woman, I am here for what's next. This. Is. History. In food justice and filmmaking!" Besaw subsequently brought nonwhite producers Par Parekh and Bernard Parham on board, postponing the release first to 2022, then to 2024. The two statements have been replaced with a joint one below a portrait of Jenkins – now credited as co-producer – and one of Besaw, who is co-director. "We have spent the last six years documenting the reality of a community negatively impacted by discrimination and injustices dating back to enslavement and compounded by the politics of racism and misogynoir that still exists today," it explains. "The creation of the ROOTED film brought together a Black and white women in a journey of listening, trust, mutual respect, growth and empowerment to call attention to everyday injustices our society tolerates and to open the minds and hearts of those pushed to the margins."

Whether it should be welcomed or regretted that *Rooted* got (temporarily) stopped in its tracks due to concerns about the allocation of narrative agency is a question I cannot answer here – more insight into the creative process would be needed. Judging from the filmmakers' joined statement, they have embraced the experience as an opportunity for cooperative learning. The reason why I have included it in my discussion of food justice narratives is that it exemplifies the potential limitations imposed by certain media forms, such as documentaries. Due to digitalization, filmmaking has become cheaper and in combination with crowd-funding schemes this has led to a democratization of the medium (Işıkman 2018), making it more accessible for low-income or otherwise marginalized communities (Monani 2013). While these are exciting developments, the production of feature-length films nevertheless necessitates a skillset as well as money and the time to plan, shoot, edit, distribute, and promote the finished product. It seems likely that Jenkins could have found a nonwhite director bringing all those qualities to her project, but this filmmaker, too, might have been an outsider to her community. If we can believe her published statement, she regretted the stalling of the film's release in 2020, although her farm continues to exist without the publicity push it might have afforded her at a crucial moment in her fight for food justice. Visiting Fresh Future Farm's website today, one finds a range of resources including videos on gardening and cooking as well as a virtual education series entitled "Fresh Future Fridays." Jenkins also joined the podcast NextBite for a three-part series about change-makers on the farm and to explain how it has met the needs of Chicora-Cherokee/Cherokee (NextBite 2021). She is still raising funds in the hope of getting a title for the land she farms, and perhaps the long delayed release of the film will help her reach that goal. For the time being she has not only succeeded in securing it but also found ways to tell her story across multiple media channels that are more easily accessible to her and her community.

What it means to own the land one farms *and* claim the narrative agency to tell its story is exemplified by another Black food justice activist who is featured in Besaw's film: Leah Penniman. The same recognitions that drove Jenkins to establish the Fresh Future Farm in a vacant lot in North Charleston led Penniman to found Soul Fire Farm outside Albany, New York. However, unlike Jenkins, Penniman was able to purchase the land. As she explains in her book, *Farming While Black*, she used to live with her husband, Jonah, and their two children, in the South End of Albany, "a neighborhood classified as a 'food desert' by the federal government" (2018, 3). After years of getting their vegetables from a community-supported agriculture (CSA) share, they had saved enough money to buy four acres of land, and "with the support of hundreds of volunteers and after four years of building infrastructure and soil," they opened Soul Fire Farm, "a project committed to ending racism and injustice in the food system, providing life-giving food to people living in food deserts, and transferring skills and knowledge to the next generation of farmer-activists" (4).[25] *Farming While Black* is her memoir, manifesto, history, and practical guide rolled all in one, providing readers "with a concise how-to for all aspects of small-scale farming, from business planning to preserving the harvest" (9). In terms of environmental, health, and food justice, Penniman minces no words when it comes to the intersections of class and race in the U.S.:

> American Racism is built into the DNA of the US food system. Beginning with the genocidal land theft from Indigenous people, continuing with the kidnapping of our ancestors from the shores of West Africa for forced agricultural labor, morphing into convict leasing, expanding to the migrant guestworker program, and maturing into its current state where farm management is among the whitest professions, farm labor is predominantly Brown and exploited, and people of color disproportionately live in food apartheid neighborhoods and suffer from diet-related illness, this system is built on stolen land and stolen labor, and needs a redesign. (5)

Such redesigning is what Penniman attempts not only through her agricultural work on the Soul Fire Farm and its many on-site outreach and education projects, but also by using a variety of interconnected media channels to convey its space and multiracial community to audiences who cannot visit in person.

Even more than Jenkins's, Penniman's work exemplifies what Donna Hancox calls *transmedia activism*. "An often overlooked aspect of transmedia storytelling," Hancox explains, "is its capacity to illuminate the relationships between people, places and practices that can influence social change, which is precisely what creators and activists have continued to strive to harness in projects" (2021). Penniman's Soul Fire Farm storyworld is a perfect example, as it is anchored in place and the "lived experiences of those who inhabit it" (Hancox 2021). The farm's website informs that it "is an Afro-Indigenous centered community farm and training center dedicated to uprooting racism and seeding sovereignty in the food system." It offers information on the

---

[25] Community-supported agriculture (CSA) is "a food production and distribution system that directly connects farmers and consumers . . . . People buy 'shares' of a farm's harvest in advance and then receive a portion of the crops as they're harvested" (Penniman 2018, 10). The system was proposal by Booker T. Whatley and other professors at Tuskegee to make Black agriculture more community-supported and sustainable.

eighty acres of farmland that "that historically was stewarded by the Stockbridge-Munsee Band of the Mohican Nation," which now is sharing seeds and working on a "cultural respect easement" with the farmers Aside from relating historical and cultural contexts, the website informs about community farm days and training programs, and it offers a host of free online resources along with links to the farm's social media. Penniman's books, which are also featured, provide the philosophy behind the project and explain the Black origins of community-supported and regenerative agriculture.[26] A "Land Skillshare Video Series" on YouTube gives practical advice to "Black, Indigenous, Latinx, and other people of color farmers and land stewards." Visitors can also enter the transmedial storyworld via the "Ask A Sista Farmer" show on Instagram Live, or the farm's newsletter. In a much more extensive way than Jenkins, Penniman's team invites visitors to explore and actively engage with the core narrative behind the Soul Fire Farm through interconnected stories in different formats and media that all weave together into a larger nonfiction storyworld about reclaiming Black agricultural heritage and working toward food justice and sovereignty. They are also invited to donate, visit, or volunteer on the farm.

In 2023, Penniman added another piece to this interactive transmedial storyworld. After collaborating over years with the filmmaker Mark Decena, she now stars in a documentary film based on *Farming While Black*, directed by Decena and produced by his company Kontent Films. While adaptations of nonfiction books are rare, they require the same kind of transmediation and contraction as other adaptations. The film thus zeroes in on a topic that is also prominent in the book: Black land ownership. "Black farmers," Penniman explains to her intended audience of Black viewers, "experienced the peak in our landownership in 1910 not because of 'forty acres and a mule' but because of saving money for two generations and purchasing 16 million acres of land. Today, ninety-eight percent of the farmland is controlled by white folks, and I think our generation is realizing that a piece of our culture and a piece of our soul was lost in that red clay. And we're now in a position to go back." Her words are accompanied by a collage of images showing her and her family on the Soul Fire Farm, working the land they own and share with other nonwhite farmers, embracing one another, boldly facing the camera. The very existence of the film is a testament to the fact that the medium of documentary film can be seamlessly integrated into a larger storyworld without giving up narrative agency. While Penniman did not direct and thus had to leave many creative choices to Decena

---

[26] Penniman also traces regenerative agriculture back to Booker T. Whatley's work at Tuskegee.

(who also features two other farmers in it), it is one more way for her to tell a piece of her story about the need for Black farmers to return to and reclaim the land.

Conclusion

In his contribution to *Utopian Foodways* (2019, 25), renowned utopian studies scholar Lyman Tower Sargent singles out Penniman's Soul Fire Farm as an example of a real-life project informed by both ancient African wisdom and utopian reach and thus as a pertinent illustration of "what is possible with a vision of a better life." After all, the community-supported and regenerative agricultural practices she advocates have been recognized as important tools not only in the fight for food justice but also in addressing pressing ecological problems such as soil degradation and climate change.[27] Aside from its rediscovery of Black agricultural heritage, it is the focus on "what it takes to bring those aspirations to life" (E.O. Wright 2007, 37) that makes not only Penniman's practical work and education efforts on the Soul Fire Farm but also her transmedial storytelling such a compelling example of a "real utopia" sustained by all four pathways toward radical hope (Mosley et al. 2020): Not only does the Soul Fire Farm educate about the history of oppression along with the actions of resistance taken to transform these conditions, it also embraces ancestral pride and envisions equitable possibilities. Finally, it seeks to create meaning and purpose in life by adopting an orientation to social, environmental, and food justice.

Jenkins and Penniman are not the only Black farmers who are raising their voices across multiple media channels to tell radically hopeful stories about food justice and sovereignty. The D-Town Farm in Detroit and the related Detroit Black Community Food Security Network now have sophisticated websites that engage visitors through a variety of media channels. Another example is "Gangsta Gardener" Ron Finley, who started out in 2010 by taking a gardening class and planting vegetables on a "parkway" dirt strip in front of his home in South Los Angeles – and promptly was cited for gardening without a permit. After starting a petition with other gardeners in his community, Finley fought for the right to use public spaces to grow food with the result that the city changed its law. In 2013, he gave a TED talk that went viral and made him an instant celebrity. Today, he runs the Ron Finley Project complete with a website, Facebook page, and YouTube channel. Notably, he rejects the notion of "giving

---

[27] Regenerative agriculture "restores and maintains soil health and fertility, supports biodiversity, protects watersheds, and improves ecological and economic resilience." Its practices serve to re-carbonize "soils via photosynthesis and biology, particularly on degraded land" and thus can "sequester increasing quantities of atmospheric carbon (CO2) underground" (C. White 2020, 799).

people hope," because "you can't do nothing with hope, but hope. But guess what you can do with *opportunity?*" However, this rejection appears to be based on an understanding of hope that lacks the crucial element of *agency* and thus is closer to wishful thinking. Finley's insistence on the central importance of opportunity nevertheless raises an important point about the need for an imaginary opening. It is this future-oriented and ultimately utopian dimension of food justice that I have explored in this chapter, along with the ways in which filmmakers and activists are using different modes of storytelling to engage and activate audiences.

As the Academy Award nomination for *The Garden* and many other awards and accolades demonstrate, impact-oriented feature documentaries meant for theatric release and/or streaming platforms should not be underestimated in their ability to attract attention and engage wide audiences. Yet, aside from their historical contingency and the practical need for bounded storytelling, they can raise complex questions around representation. In this chapter, I have sought to demonstrate that such films have nevertheless been integrated into the larger transmedia storyworlds of food justice activists, and that the distribution of narrative agency can be more fluent than is often acknowledged. As we will see in the second part of *Growing Hope*, such narrative integration and fluidity have also been a valuable tool for activists who focus less on equal *access* to fresh and healthy food and more on what people heap onto their plates.

Especially interesting in this context is the way in which prominent food justice activists are dealing with difficult questions surrounding the production and consumption of meat, along with related concerns about health, ethics, and ecological sustainability. Toward the end of *Farming While Black*, Penniman states that she voluntarily kills "hundreds of chickens every year," even though she herself is a "flexible" vegetarian, because she knows that "our community eats meat, and I want that meat to be humanely and sustainably raised" (2018, 167), before proceeding to give detailed, step-by-step instructions (including illustrations) for killing chickens while making the dying animal as comfortable as possible. In the final section of the chapter, entitled "Meat and Sustainability," Penniman acknowledges that "industrial livestock production is an environmental justice disaster, adversely impacting communities of color" as well as an environmental disaster (179). "At the same time," she states, "meat is part of our cultural heritage and ancestral cuisine" (180), a dilemma she hopes to solve with organically raised animals and smaller portions of their meat. Some food justice activists have challenged precisely this assumption. The narratives I will consider in the second part – "Eat: Narrating Vegan Food Justice" – look at these issues through the lens of *vegan* food justice. Fully on board with improving people's access to fruit and vegetables, they suggest that living a healthier and better life while showing compassion for other beings and respect for the ecosystems that sustain us, necessitates decolonizing both the SAD and people's understanding of veganism.

EAT: NARRATING VEGAN FOOD JUSTICE

3 Decolonizing Veganism

A few minutes into Jasmine Leyva's 2019 documentary *The Invisible Vegan*, the filmmaker sits on a porch overlooking a garden and relates a story reminiscent of Leah Penniman's at the beginning of *Farming While Black*, but with an important twist. If it was organic agriculture and environmental stewardship that Penniman thought Black people did not care about when she was young, Levya tells viewers that she used to think veganism was "a white thing." In fact, she did not even know it existed. "I grew up in DC eating the Standard American Diet," she explains, "meat, dairy, fruit, veggies, bread. . . . My entire family eats meat, so that's what I knew, and it's all I knew." By the time Levya became a teenager, she had heard of vegetarianism, but it was only when she moved to Los Angeles at the age of twenty that she learned about veganism and that it was for white people. Then, she witnessed an interview with Babette Davis, the then-65-year-old owner of the plant-based restaurant Stuff I Eat. Seeing the fit body and young-looking face of a much older Black woman who was very vocal about the benefits of veganism made a deep impression on Levya, so much so that she went vegan herself.

Davis has been an influential figure because she went vegan in the 1990s at a time when few people did so, almost none of them Black. It is only in recent years that veganism has started to reach the American mainstream, fueled by ethical, environmental, and health-related concerns (L. Wright 2019, ix). As a result, the variety of plant-based products and their sales have risen steeply (Forgrieve 2018). In the big coastal cities, most supermarkets and many restaurants cater to the growing number of people who are adding vegan dishes to their diet. Prominent vegans such as Joachim Phoenix, Woody Harrelson, Ava DuVernay, and Venus Williams are further propagating the trend. Quite a few of them are Black, and Black Americans are in fact more likely than white Americans to identify as vegans (Stahler & Mangels 2022). However, that has not changed much about the widespread perception of veganism as white, middle-class, and female in mainstream discourse, a portrayal that reproduces ideas of whiteness that stand in direct opposition to the actual demographic data of vegans living in the U.S. (Shah 2018). This is an unduly limited understanding that overlooks the many ways in which veganism can contribute to Black liberation as well as to discourses around food justice and multispecies justice.[28] Jessica Holmes's observation bears repeating here: "Veganism continues to be largely overlooked as a rights-based social justice movement in the interests of both human and nonhuman animals, too often being regarded as a restrictive dietary and/or (at best) lifestyle preference" (2021, 178). Levya acknowledges that limited understanding in her documentary while arguing that veganism is *not* at odds with Black existential needs, political priorities, or cherished culinary traditions such as Soul Food. She uses her voice as a Black vegan woman to urge other African Americans to reject the food narratives they have been fed for centuries and switch to plant-based diets that are culturally appropriate, accessible, and affordable. To use a term proposed by scholars such as A. Breeze Harper (2010) and Jennifer Polish (2016) and food justice activists such as Luz Calvo and Catriona Rueda (2015): they must learn to *decolonize* their diets.

As we have seen in Part I, one important strategy of food justice activism has been to improve access by growing vegetables locally and inviting the community to join, the underlying assumption being that this will automatically improve their eating habits and physical health. As Malik Yakini puts it in Todd Darling's film *Urban Roots*, "People tend to eat what they have access to. And if what people have access to are prepackaged, frozen, canned foods but don't have easy access to fresh produce, then they will tend to eat those things that they have access to." Empirical evidence suggests that, to a degree, this is true and in part related to people's perception of their food environment (Karpyn et al. 2020). However, it must not necessarily mean that giving people access to fresh fruit and vegetables will automatically lead them to eat healthier diets (Dibsdall et al. 2003). While there are studies showing that improved access does correlate with increased consumption (Caldwell et al. 2008), there are also those suggesting that moral, cultural, and identity-related factors play an important role in what people choose to eat, regardless of access (Carter 2021; Widener 2018).[29] In this and the next chapter, I will look at a selection of nonfiction narratives that interrogate such factors from a vegan food justice perspective.

Vegan studies scholar Laura Wright positions veganism itself as a disruptive opposition to the capitalist exploitation of animals and people (2017 727). However, the narratives I have selected are invested in destigmatizing veganism

---

[28] On the relationship between veganism and multispecies justice, see Vegan Justice Collective (2024).

[29] It is more difficult to establish a clear relationship between improved access to fruit and vegetables and improved health, but the physical work in an urban garden has been shown to have a positive effect (Cano-Verdugo 2024).

for nonwhite communities and elevating the voices of people of color dedicated to freeing their own lives and those of their communities from the detrimental influence of unhealthy food traditions and the industrial agricultural complex. It is in this way that their work intersects with that of the community farmer-activists I discussed in the preceding chapters. As Teagan Murphy and Anne Mook state, vegan scholars of color highlight that a full commitment to veganism is not only informed by health and ethical concerns, but it "is simultaneously a commitment to dismantling white supremacy" (2022, 4). Vegan food justice is only complete when it combines the fight for equitable access to fresh produce with a healthier diet and a concern for the rights and well-being of nonhuman animals and the environment.

I will start my exploration with a look at A. Breeze Harper's groundbreaking anthology, *Sistah Vegan* (2010), which collects the personal stories of Black vegan women aiming to decolonize their bodies from heavily processed and unhealthy diets and their minds from patriarchal, racist, and speciesist ideologies. I will also consider Aph Ko and Syl Ko's *Aphro-ism* (2017), which interrogates the emergence of radical hope at the intersection of race, feminism, and the advocacy for nonhuman animals. In the second section, I will return to Leyva's *The Invisible Vegan* and examine it as an autobiographical documentary made by a Black woman and first-time filmmaker who claims narrative agency to speak about her personal journey to veganism in combination with a deeper look at systemic racism and the unhealthy dietary patterns in the African American community. The conclusion will shift the focus to vegan Black men and their storytelling in *Sistah Vegan*'s more recent companion book, Omowale Adewale's *Brotha Vegan* (2021). In all these stories, veganism is understood as a form of embodied resistance to a colonizing food system "that has historically perpetuated food insecurity within many low-income communities of color" (Murphy & Mook 2022, 4). As such, it "serves as a mechanism to reject both the speciesism and racism of colonized food systems," and thus is a crucial contribution to the narrativization of food justice.

Food for Thought: Decolonizing Diets in *Sistah Vegan* and *Aphro-ism*

Starting from her own conflicted response to a controversial campaign ad created by PETA (People for the Ethical Treatment of Animals), Breeze Harper sets out to explore what it means to be vegan as a Black woman in the U.S. In her introduction to *Sistah Vegan* (2010, xiv), she contextualizes PETA's "Animal Liberation Project" ad, which jarringly juxtaposes human suffering and animal suffering (C. Kim 2011), with a quote from Marjorie Spiegel's *The Dreaded Comparison* (1996, 30). "As divergent as the cruelties and supporting systems of oppression may be," Spiegel argues, "there are commonalities between" the oppression experienced by Black people and by animals. Noting that PETA was sharply criticized by the Black community for the insensitivity of the comparison, she suggests reexamining the project of veganism "from a Black feminist, antiracist, and decolonizing perspective" (2010, xv). The result of that endeavor, which first took the form of an online forum that later resulted in the anthology, is the exploration of four interrelated questions about (1) Black women's use of veganism to decolonize their bodies and engage in health activism that resists institutionalized racism and neocolonialism; (2) their reactions to depictions of vegans "as mostly white and thin;" (3) the degree to which they perceive veganism as "being part of a legacy of white racism and an elitist view of culinary ideologies," and (4) how it might nevertheless be presented as a tool that simultaneously resists institutionalized racism, environmental degradation, and "high rates of health dis-eases plaguing the Black community" (xv).

The original idea for the forum was prompted by Harper's own "experiences with institutionalized racism, heterosexualism, and sexism" (xvii), and by her sociological research as a PhD student at UC Davis. The first, after dealing with health problems and reading books by Queen Afua and the civil rights movement icon Dick Gregory, led her to adopt "*ahimsa*-based veganism."[30] The second led to an understanding of "how horrible the state of health is among the Black female population" due to eating "too much junk food and not enough fruit and vegetables," along with an addiction to "postindustrialized Soul Food practices" (xviii–xix).[31] The *Sistah Vegan* online forum was a way for Harper to explore with other Black female vegans how to deal with the threat that food is posing to the health of their communities. At the same time, adopting a vegan diet in a society that normalizes and subsidizes the consumption of industrially produced animal products added more layers of emotional turmoil and discrimination for women of color that intersected with the sexism and racism they were already experiencing (Rawlins 2021). Turning these conversations into a book meant lifting them out of the safe online space in which it had developed to widen the circle of those who could learn and think about these perspectives on Black female veganism. As Harper puts it at the end of her introduction, "it's nice to finally be at the table with some food for thought" (2010, xix). And there is plenty of it.

---

[30] Harper explains that the veganism she practices is based on the concept of *ahimsa,* meaning "a life of practicing noninjury or harmlessness to *all* living beings" (2010, xvii), as taught by Indian philosopher Jiddu Krishnamurti.

[31] With reference to data published by the American Heart Association and the American Cancer Society regarding high rates of cardiovascular diseases, obesity, and diabetes among Black Americans, Harper notes that "Soul Food (a.k.a. Southern home-cooking or comfort food) is often jokingly referred to as a 'heart-attack on plate' (2010, 6).

The stories collected in *Sistah Vegan* are remarkable for their self-reflexivity and candidness, and it is disheartening how often they mention social isolation and ostracism within the Black community. "It's lonely being a vegan in a world where ninety-nine percent aren't," writes Delicia Durham. "The world can even be lonelier for a vegan if you're Black and female. And our … cultures are typically far from supportive of the life we have been called to lead" (2010, 42). Melissa Danielle reports that many Black people in her community "proceed to 'educate' [her] on the traditional Black diet," reminding her that she is "not a true member of the race for not eating pork," a central ingredient of traditional Soul Food (2010, 47). When she tries to inform them about the health benefits of a vegan diet, they walk away. As Harper points out, "Soul Food has been rooted in how many Black-identified people embrace or define their 'Blackness'" (2010, 21), and so they feel unsettled by the suggestion that it might be detrimental to their health and others' well-being (Carter 2021, 83). One way to address such fears has been to decolonize Soul Food by historicizing its origins – this is a point I will return to. However, it is not only the food itself that is often constructed as alien to Black culture, but also veganism's ethical stance on animals. Ain Drew relates that working at PETA as a Black woman in the early 2000s meant she was "reprimanded by members of my own community for holding my position … . how dare I campaign against the diets of our foremothers and forefathers?" (2010, 61). Time and again, the contributors to *Sistah Vegan* speak of the same preconceptions within the Black community: that veganism is an elitist practice for middle-class white women, and that Black people cannot go vegan without betraying their own traditions and history.

While the contributions are heterogenous and the perspectives remarkably diverse, their resistance to such preconceptions tends to come from the authors' own value systems and the knowledge they have gained by educating themselves, especially when it comes to the suffering of nonhuman animals and the health benefits of a whole-food plant-based diet. "The diets of my foremothers and forefathers," writes Drew, "kept bellies full in a time when opportunity to maintain a healthy lifestyle was extremely limited. In many low-income areas, they still do … . This perpetual cycle keeps the community down, stricken with high cholesterol, obesity, and suffering from conditions that could be easily avoided" (2010, 63). This is why she was appalled by PETA's decision to opt for the "shock tactics" for their "The Animal Liberation Project" ad, which "didn't directly address the health issues of the community they were trying so badly to reach" (64). Unless this changes on a broader cultural level, going vegan as a Black woman will continue to mean, as Venus Taylor puts it, "choosing to trust yourself over the teaching of men, doctors, ministers, white people, and other Black folk" (2010, 60). However, while that might have been a fruitful strategy for "decolonizing" individual female Black bodies in the first decade of the twenty-first century, it leaves those bodies isolated and without the comfort, support, and agency of a community.

Moreover, as Jennifer Polish has argued, it is not only individual Black bodies and food traditions that can and should be decolonized but also veganism itself: "Though whiteness currently taints much of vegan rhetoric and activism, it does not *need* to, and therefore the status quo of mainstream vegan whiteness *can* be decolonized and overturned" (2016, 377). Melissa Danielle speaks to this potential for decolonization in her contribution to *Sistah Vegan*, where she argues that "collectively, we can embrace [veganism] as more than just a change in our way of eating. It is a political statement, another weapon in our fight for economic, social, and political empowerment" (2010, 48). In fact, it has even larger implications that extend beyond the human realm, as Harper observes in her own contribution to the book, because "eco-sustainability, nonhuman animal rights, plant-based diets, and human rights *are* inextricably linked" (2010, 20; emphasis in original). Unfortunately, however, the health and consumption practices of Black Americans "are frequently contradictory to our social justice beliefs, in the Black community as well as other communities engaged in antiracist and antipoverty social justice work in the U.S." (22). The problem, for Harper, is not only that African Americans have become addicted to foods that are not healthy for them, but that these acquired tastes are contributing to the abuse and killing of billions of animals, which effectively puts them "in collusion with environmental racism and cultural genocide of our own brown and Black indigenous brothas and sistahs" as well as "the working poor, globally and locally" (27–28). In this understanding, food justice taken seriously *must* be vegan food justice, and veganism without an expressed concern for food justice is morally problematic and politically harmful.

One insight offered by *Sistah Vegan*'s chorus of voices is that veganism is a particularly challenging diet and lifestyle for Black women because it appears to be at odds with Black culture and food traditions. Meanwhile, it is precisely this tradition and related culinary desires that contribute to the food and health justice issues impacting Black Americans. As pattrice jones notes in her Afterword to *Sistah Vegan*, the "anthology demonstrates the necessity of decolonizing *desire*, not only among formerly colonized peoples but among all of us whose socially constructed appetites are eating up the world" (2010, 188; emphasis mine). Decolonizing culinary desire is not easy, but jones frames it as a necessity: "desire for the steaks and shakes and deep-fried mystery meats that clog the arteries of so many African Americans might best be seen as a form of literally internalized colonialism. And now come the sistah vegans asking other Black people to recognize their appetites as potential artifacts of white colonial rule" (196–197). Returning to the controversial PETA campaign and Spiegel's *The Dreaded Comparison* that Harper evoked at the beginning of the book, jones emphasizes the moral *complicity* involved in "coming to desire dead bodies for dinner" and notes that "the contributors to this anthology are united in their answer to complicity: integrity," and thus the striving for "for actions that are consistent with beliefs" (2010, 187). Like Harper, she encourages an understanding of veganism that takes on board not only concerns about food justice but also anti-speciesist ethics without losing sight of Black liberation.

Sistah Vegan served as important inspiration for many other Black-identifying female vegans, among them the sisters Aph and Syl Ko, whose book of essays, *Aphro-ism,* offers a feminist and critical race approach to vegan food justice that sets out to challenge precisely the narrative that anti-speciesism and Black liberation are incompatible. As they write in their Author's Note, the Ko sisters turned to writing to "work out our frustrations and confusion, our ideas and hopes, and our suggestions for a better, more empathetic world" (2017, n.p.). In fact, an entire chapter of the book is dedicated to *confusion* as a necessary precondition for the development of meaningful and effective vegan food justice activism. "Part of activism," postulates Aph Ko, "is finding yourself in a new space of confusion" (2017, 28). Abandoning commonly held oppressive beliefs, she explains, can put one in a spot "where you might not exactly know what to do afterward, and that's where more activists need to be" because it means "allowing yourself to step into new conceptual terrain" (28). This is why *Aphro-ism* is conceived as a conversation, organized into alternating chapters that are written by one or, in some cases, both Ko sisters, and dedicated to topics from a critique of the normalization of whiteness to a reminder that pointing out commonalities between the oppressed and the oppressor will not necessarily end the oppression, regardless of whether the oppressed is human or animal. "Like many vegans of color doing justice work for nonhuman animals and human beings," explains Breeze Harper in her Foreword for the book (2017, n.p.), "Syl and Aph critically but compassionately narrate their challenges in being anti-racist and black feminist scholars amongst people of color who do not politicize animality" and mainstream animal liberation movements pursuing "post-racial" approaches to justice and freedom for nonhuman animals.

Black veganism, in the words of Syl Ko, "is a methodological tool to reactivate our imaginations" (2017, 126), because it recognizes that "racism is simultaneously anti-*black* and anti-*animal*, as seen by racial ideology's elevation and celebration of 'the human' and 'humanity' particularly as Western and *white*" (121). Racial politics, she makes clear, has long been structured along the animal-human division whereby the white human male takes the superior position and with increasing distance both the subjugation and attribution of animality increases. Dismantling this oppressive narrative is a crucial step in the process of decolonization, one that necessitates a rethinking of the argument that "people of color are humans, too; so, we should treat them as humans, not animals" because doing so involves "an open acceptance of the negative status of 'the animal'" and thus "a tacit acceptance of the hierarchical racial system of white supremacy in general" (45). Yet, Black veganism also involves a commitment to anti-racism, which is where it departs from much of mainstream veganism. As Carol Adams writes in her Afterword to the book, "The problem is that some Eurocentric vegans never perceived dismantling racism as part of their mandate" (2017, 141). Black veganism propagates a "multidimensional" understanding of shared oppressions (Ko 2019, 119), hoping that drawing attention to the conceptual and invented roots of both racism *and* speciesism will allow it to retain its radically hopeful political potential.

How much the sisters' work in *Aphro-isms* is rooted in radical hope rather than just a desire for change is evident in the fact that it ends with this quote from Ytasha Womack's *Afrofuturism* (2013, 42):

> Hope, much like imagination, comes at a premium. The cost is a life where more is expected. Where more is expected, new actions are required. The audacity of hope, the bold declaration to believe, and clarity of vision for a better life and world are the seeds to personal growth, revolutionized societies, and life-changing technologies.

The Ko sisters refrain from elaborating, letting the quote stand for itself. However, ending with the audacity of hope gives their book at once a utopian horizon and an air of real possibility. The focus on personal growth and transformation also resonates with their earlier insistence on the need to "step into new conceptual terrain" (2017, 28) and with pattrice jones's observation that the contributors to *Sistah Vegan* tell "over and over again . . . of discordance leading to discomfort leading to change" (2010, 187). By underlining the agency-component of hope, Womack reminds us that it requires and engenders *action*. The types of action might be manifold – one might go vegan, plant a garden, join a protest, or, as Jasmine Levya has done, make a film to elevate her own voice along with the voices of other Black vegans.

From Black Lives Matter to Veganism: Jasmine Leyva's *The Invisible Vegan*

The Invisible Vegan is not only the first vegan advocacy film directed and produced by a Black female vegan – it is also Levya's first film. She shares that experience with Mark MacInnis, who was a first-time filmmaker when he made *Urban Roots*, but Levya's professional background and skillset were different when she embarked on her project. In addition to a BA in TV, Film, and Media and an MFA in screenwriting, she had several years of work in the entertainment industry under her belt when she felt ready to write and direct her own film. However, when she approached the executive producer of the TV show she was working on, she hit a wall that most first-time filmmakers know well. Rather than letting herself get discouraged by the rejection, Levya remembers it as the moment "it hit" her: "I cannot keep waiting for someone else to give me the go to pursue my own passion. I have to use the resources at my disposal and make it happen" (Scoop Interview 2021). While not romanticizing the daunting experience of first fundraising and then shooting, producing, and promoting a feature-length documentary film on a small budget, she admits that she is proud of claiming narrative agency. As Alicia Smith-Tran has noted, *The Invisible Vegan* "provides thoughtful insights into both the health benefits of veganism and … the complexities of food consumption among Black Americans and the structures that enable and constrain choices" (2020). It is this combination that makes the film an interesting food justice narrative.

Compared to *Urban Roots* and the other films I have discussed, *The Invisible Vegan* is rougher around the edges stylistically and a lot more personal, combining elements of the autobiographical documentary with those of the expository mode. While Kennedy, Darling, and MacInnis are almost never seen in their films, Leyva does not shy away from getting up close and personal. This is typical for the autobiographical mode of documentary film, which often also "embraces and is inflected by the political" (Renov 2008, 49), and, since it can be realized on a relatively modest budget, is more accessible than other media forms to those who want to advocate and mobilize "social, cultural, political and legal change" (French 2019). *The Invisible Vegan* uses archival footage to chart Levya's life trajectory from a child cherishing her grandmother's breakfasts of "sausage, eggs, and fluffy butter biscuits" to a young woman who has grown critical of such traditional Soul Food. The first impulse for that transformation came from her encounter with Babette Davis, which led her to read up on veganism and try out vegan recipes that, in the film, her friends flippantly call "white people's food." Levya has acknowledged that her main target audience for the film is other Black Americans who are skeptical about veganism and that the goal of her film is to "promote the diet … in a way that is not elitist and offensive" (Scoop 2021). Her often playful approach to her own and other's preconceptions is meant to make the experience more relatable for this audience.

However, *The Invisible Vegan* also has elements of the expository mode, offering testimonies from Black health experts and food scholars such as Psyche Williams-Forson, who explains that Black Americans "have a very vexed relationship with food ... because we've been told that we eat 'low on the hog;'" however, "to associate veganism and vegetarianism with whiteness, you are totally discounting our cultural heritage." Milton Mills, a medical doctor and Associate Director of Preventive Medicine at PCRM, explains that "traditional West African diets ... are plant-based, low in fat, and also contain very little meat. West Africans who were used to eating this diet" were "dragged from their homes, shipped across the ocean, and then confined to plantations where they were literally fed the garbage of the plantation." Levya relates this to her own former ignorance, stating that she had not realized that her "ancestors came from a rich land with rich soil .... All I knew was 'we turned scraps into Soul Food.'" The interplay between autobiographical and expert voices seeks to educate viewers about their precolonial and colonial culinary legacies and then reminds them of famous Black vegetarians and vegans such as Rosa Parks, Angela Davis, and Dick Gregory to challenge their understanding of those legacies.

Autobiographical documentaries can raise important questions about the relationship and distribution of narrative agency between filmmaker and subjects (Dowmunt 2013, 263), and so it bears mentioning that Levya frames her own experiences of being "not Black enough" because of her food choices with those of other Black vegans such as nutritionist Tracye McQuirter – whose influential blog, *By Any Greens Necessary*, I will discuss in Chapter 4 – and writer and activist Sebastian McJetters, who asks "why should your Black card be forfeit because you decided that your health and wellness is not predicated on ... animal proteins or putting animal secretions in your body? Your Black card should be contingent on your commitment to Black liberation." Levya illustrates McJetters words with graphic images of animal slaughter before proposing to *reimagine* Soul Food to "preserve our legacy and still be healthy" – an important point I will also return to. From here, the film takes time to demonstrate the negative health implications associated with a traditional Soul Food diet, such as heart disease, obesity, and diabetes, but it does refrain from blaming Black individuals for their poor health. Harper, who is also featured in the film, states that "it is popular in the mainstream vegan movement to ... promote veganism as a cure-all, making people feel as if it's the individual's responsibility to take control of their health, and it really ignores a lot of the systemic factors that make it difficult for a lot of people." The film thus shifts to the important topic of *access*, shedding light on how difficult it is to adopt a healthy, whole-food vegan diet in low-income neighborhoods that have turned into food deserts. This is where *The Invisible Vegan* most overtly intersects with the urban farming documentaries I have discussed, engaging with both food justice activism, represented by The Food Empowerment Project, and urban community gardening, represented by The

Green Scheme and Soilful City. The Green Scheme uses gardening "as a *weapon* to help people in the community to fight back against lack of access," Levya says in the film, suggesting that low-income communities of color must literally fight for food justice. Then, however, she asks a crucial question that connects the two parts of this Element, GROW and EAT: "So there's the issue of access, but let's say more people in marginalized communities had access to healthy food, would they eat it?"

Her answer to this question is appropriately complex and takes into consideration several cultural factors, most centrally the inextricably linked nature of gender and race. As Smith-Tran points out, these segments of the film "explore the ways in which raced gender expectations and gender performances are oppressive for both Black men and Black women" (2020, 374), highlighting that plant-based ways of eating are often perceived as contrary to dominant norms of masculinity. Levya thus uses the medium of documentary film to thematize an issue that transcends the Black community, and that Carol Adams encapsulated in her observation that, in American culture, "meat eating is a male activity" (1990, 26). Alex Lockwood reminds us that food choices are part of a larger "socially constructed narrative we call masculinity," which "is a major factor in why men fail to learn how to process emotions, refuse to get cancer screening . . . or consume certain kinds of food (such as meat) and eschew others (such as 'effemiate' or vegan foods)" (2021, 295). *The Invisible Vegan* participates in a discourse that also informs another vegan advocacy film, Louie Psihoyos's *The Game Changers* (2018), about the physical prowess and sexual potency of vegan athletes – or "hegans" as Laura Wright calls men who "are so ultramasculine as to be able to be vegan and to make that dietary choice manly as well" (2015, 126). However, Levya's film also presents a more flexible path for male-identifying vegans and those who are considering such a choice. The film thus resonates in important ways with *Sistah Vegan*'s more recent companion book, Omowale Adewale's *Brotha Vegan* (2021), which offers "a profound rethinking of the meaning of veganism" (17) from the perspective of Black men. Such examination is needed, argues Adewale in his introduction to the anthology, since in a society that associates masculinity with meat eating and veganism with white femininity, Black male vegans are "the antitheses of what might be 'expected' of men (particularly heterosexual men), and doubly antithetical to expectations surrounding Black men" (14). Even more so than Black women, they must either continue living as "invisible vegans" or challenge, expand, and decolonize the very concept of veganism. *The Invisible Vegan* does not shy away from these gender troubles, and Levya deliberately made room in her film for the voices of non-vegan Black men who struggle with the idea of going plant-based, and those who are vegan, like McJetters, and are trying to shift Black veganism away from confining concepts of femininity *and* heteronormativity.[32]

The Invisible Vegan is thus a nuanced advocacy film not only for veganism, but also for Black liberation and environmental and food justice. In its final chapter, the documentary highlights that communities of color not only live closer to landfills and, but also to industrial cow and pig farms, which pose just as much of a danger to them. The founder of the Food Empowerment Project, Lauren Ornelas, explains that "In North Carolina you have predominantly Black communities living around pig farms where they are suffering from nose bleeds and headaches, and nausea, they can't open their windows because of the flies and the stench." A montage illustrates her words: close-ups of cow manure, a Black child on an inhalator, maggots, flies, and the cruel abuse of a small piglet that cues the kind of trans-species empathy I have discussed elsewhere (Weik von Mossner 2017, 2019). "That's why by stopping eating animal products," Ornelas says, "by not drinking that milk, by not eating any animal products you are not participating in a system that also causes harm to these communities living in these areas, which are predominantly communities of color." Those last words are spoken over an image of another Black child looking directly at the camera. Leyva's use of graphic imagery is deliberately disturbing as she drives home her point, and that of the Ko sisters, that animal rights and human rights intersect. "It's just an animal," writes Syl Ko in *Aphro-ism*, "can no longer be an excuse for treating a being as if s(he) merely existed for us. To think in that way is to participate in racial thinking" (2017, 69). In its final minutes, *The Invisible Vegan* addresses the negative effects of industrial animal agriculture on biodiversity and the climate, ending with the voice of Aph Ko over a series of black title cards, stating that "when we get people to think critically about their world, their behaviors will change as well. Talking about veganism … isn't the only way to get people to not eat meat. The reality is we all need to be thinking about this stuff because we all live on planet Earth." Whatever it takes, Levya's film ultimately suggests, whatever the reasons or motivations, we must begin to interrogate human–animal relations as part of a wider analysis of "multidimensional" oppressions (Ko 2019, 119) in a complex process of decolonizing veganism and ensuring justice for all.

---

[32] Emilia Quinn's even asserts a "specific resonance of queerness for a distinctly 'vegan' identity" which eschews moral puritanism and allows for contradictions and inconsistencies and establishes veganism "as a horizon of becoming as opposed to a state at which one can successfully arrive" (2021, 268–269).

Conclusion

Black veganism has come a long way since Breeze Harper started her online forum in 2005. She has become one of the most recognizable voices in the Black vegan community as well as in the academic field of vegan studies. In addition to her academic work, she is the author of three novels and runs the *Sistah Vegan Project Blog*. These diverse forms of storytelling – which include the voices and stories of other Black women around a common issue – allow Harper to keep adding new dimensions to her chosen core narrative about the need for vegan food justice. She has also promoted other Black vegan authors and filmmakers, as is evidenced in the fact that she wrote the Foreword for both *Aphro-ism* and *Brotha Vegan* and appears in Levya's film. Since *The Invisible Vegan* was released in 2019, the perception of veganism has continued to shift within the African American community. At the time of writing, Black Americans are not only going vegan at a higher rate than any other racial group in the United States, but their voices are also getting louder. "The more Black people go vegan," hopes McJetters in the final minutes of Levya's film, "the higher the potential is for it to become a part of the national consciousness." The books and film I have discussed in this chapter have played an important role in this process by providing platforms that empowered previously "invisible" vegans to speak out and in turn empower others.

Asked what advice she would give other women who are interested in shooting their own film about issues they care about, Levya referred to the dual enabling powers of contemporary technology and the unashamed claiming of narrative agency: "If you want to direct, produce, edit, act, and you have a smartphone you have the capabilities to shoot your own stuff, so start making your own content . . . . Don't walk around saying that want to you do something – be doing it" (Scoop Interview 2021). Aside from opportunity, the crucial ingredients of hope – positive expectations, agency, and trust – are presented as enabling factors. This is precisely the approach taken by Black vegans such as Tabitha Brown, Tracye McQuirter, Jenné Claiborne, and Bryant Terry who have built large transmedial platforms to advocate wholesome vegan lifestyles and challenge both mainstream veganism and the concept of what exactly vegan food *is* or can be. In *Sistah Vegan*, Harper quotes Dick Gregory, who famously claimed "that the quickest way to wipe out a group of people is to put them on a Soul Food diet" (2010, xxi). However, as Leyva suggests in *The Invisible Vegan*, rather than just exchanging cherished Soul Food dishes for more prosaic salads, there are ways of *reimaging* and *reinventing* the former in a way that retains aspects of its beloved taste while turning it into something plant-based and healthy. This feat has been undertaken the some of the vegan chefs and food bloggers I will consider in the next chapter, who are in the business of creating narratives and recipes for mouthwatering Soul Food dishes without losing sight of food justice.

4 Visceralizing Food Justice

In 2015, Bryant Terry gave a TEDMED talk entitled "Stirring Up Political Change from the Kitchen." Only months before assuming his new role as the Inaugural Chef-in-Residence at the Museum of the African Diaspora in San Francisco, he took the talk as an opportunity to look back at some of the choices that turned him into a vegan chef and food justice activist. Watching the recording, we learn that his family grew most of its food in its own backyard and that he developed an unhealthy addiction to fast food in high school until a hip-hop song about beef and reading Upton Sinclair's *The Jungle* made him stop eating meat. We also learn that he had embarked on a PhD program in History at NYU when two things coincided that changed the path of his life: doing research on radical movements of the 1960s and 1970s, he learned about the Black Panthers' Free Breakfast for Children Program.[33] Meanwhile, every morning on the subway, he watched "young people, children, drinking sodas, sugary juices, energy drinks, eating candy bars, salty chips, and the items from the dollar menu of fast food restaurants," and realized that "this was their breakfast." The realization was so disturbing that Terry left NYU with a master's degree and went to culinary school instead with a plan to use *cooking* as an intervention to change people's habits, attitudes, and politics around food. It is a strategy that, in the TEDMED talk, he sums up as "start with the visceral to ignite the cerebral and end with the political" and that has since informed not only his culinary work, but also the transmedial nonfiction storyworld he has created.

This chapter considers culinary texts that partake in the larger project of decolonizing veganism via a focus on food justice, which I examined in the previous chapter, but tries a more visceral approach. The work I will discuss uses the narration of cooking and food as a both practical and delightful approach to "an anti-racist vegan critique" (Navarro 2021, 282). As someone who has studied the affective strategies of environmental narratives – including vegan food narratives – for some time, I was immediately struck when I first came across Terry's mantra – "start with the visceral to ignite the cerebral and end at the political" – in his cookbook *Afro-Vegan* (2009, 318) because it captures perfectly the way in which not only material food but also the

---

[33] The Black Panthers' Free Breakfast for Children Program started in January 1969 in Oakland and spread to chapters in twenty-three American cities by the end of the year, feeding more than 20,000 children. Because of its success, it drew the suspicion of FBI Director J. Edgar Hoover. It nevertheless continued until 1980 (Pien 2010).

narratives that evoke it in the embodied minds of readers and viewers can intervene in culinary, cultural, and political discourse. I am interested in the ways in which Black vegan chefs, cookbook authors, and food bloggers appeal to their audiences' imagination – and their gut – to help them think differently about the relationship between food, health, racial justice, and empowerment.

The first section of the chapter explores how work in embodied narratology can be brought to bear on the narration of preparing, beholding, and enjoying food, looking at examples of Black vegan food bloggers and vloggers, who have created vast transmedial storyworlds around their brands. Even though vegan food blogging and vlogging continue to be dominated by white women who locate veganism "within neoliberal healthist and contemporary privileged (white) wellness imperatives" (Brown & Carruthers 2020, 87), Black vegans such as Tracye McQuirter, Tabitha Brown, and Jenné Claiborne are successfully using their websites and social media accounts along with traditionally published cookbooks, TV shows, videos, and other media, they advocate for veganism, from nutrition tips and recipes to community organizing. The second section will return to Bryant Terry's work. In an interview he gave for the *Brotha Vegan* anthology, Terry says that his "primary focus as an activist is addressing the public health crisis among African Americans that is partially driven by what we eat" (2021, 26). The way he goes about this is by seducing people with mouthwatering Soul Food recipes to get them "to cook at home and share meals with family and friends as a revolutionary first step toward food justice" (2012, loc 211). Sociologist Michael Carolan has conceptualized the visceral engagement with food as a form of "co-experimentation," highlighting the "transformative potential that lies in those sticky doings with others" (2015, 135) in an embodied practice that goes beyond mere learning. "Such attempts to re-tune our bodies, practices, and knowledge," argues Carolan, "make alternative food futures more do-able" (136–137). The Black vegan food storytellers whose work I examine in this chapter are precisely in the business of such enabling of alternative food futures.

The Transmedia Tactics of Black Vegan Nutritionists, Bloggers, and Vloggers

One of the most remarkable events in the history of Black vegan food vlogging is a three-minute video that shows Tabitha Brown in her car in a Whole Foods parking lot, eating with relish the second half of a vegan sandwich while reviewing it. It was posted in December 2017 when Brown was a struggling actress who was dealing with financial and health problems. In her review video, she nevertheless looks radiant as she gushes about the phenomenal taste of her sandwich and praises God for his blessings. The video went viral and Whole Foods promptly hired Brown as a brand ambassador; two years later, she started her own TikTok channel. By now, she has over five million followers on the platform as well as three million followers on Facebook, four million on Instagram, and a few hundred thousand on whatever is left of Twitter/X. Moreover, in a development that has become typical for successful social media influencers, she by now has also published four books through traditional trade presses as well as her own shows in places like YouTube, the Ellen Digital Channel, and the Food Network. No matter which medium she uses, Brown presents the same bubbly persona: a woman who cannot believe all the good things God has provided for her while whipping up easy and colorful vegan recipes without any political comment.

Given that Brown is also an entrepreneur with her own line of beauty products and range of spices who has struck deals with large corporations such as Target, she arguably participates in what Eva Giraud calls "the commodification of veganism": the rise of plant-based capitalism due to "the actions of corporations who have seen the potential of new vegan markets" (2021, 135). Yet regardless of whether one celebrates the success of the Black vegan influencer without reservations or is concerned about possible corporate co-optation, it is a fact that Brown's cheerful persona and nonjudgmental attitude toward other people's food choices ("Because that's your business"), has resonated with millions of followers, readers, and viewers across numerous media platforms. She is one of several Black vegans who have taken advantage of the fact that vlogging on social media like TikTok and Instagram can provide access and visibility to marginalized identities, allowing them to integrate culturally diverse vegan practices into otherwise mainstream food content (Lang 2021). Moreover, despite her conscious decision to focus on joy, she also uses her platform to speak up about anti-Black racism and advocate activism. "I've experienced more racism in my lifetime than I can count," she has shared with her followers. "Racism is a pandemic, and we have to find a cure. We all must do our part." She has also acknowledged that "women are still fighting for equality. And as a Black woman, the fight is even harder" (quoted in Bowie 2020). Even in such moments, however, she is consistent in her appearance and appeal, choosing "to spread love while spreading awareness!" In a corner of the internet that is "typically dominated by young, thin, white women – vegan content, self-improvement and TikTok more broadly" (Lang 2021), she advocates for a race-conscious, spiritual veganism with a near-complete focus on positive emotions such as love and joy.

Her remarkable success notwithstanding, Brown is far from the only Black vegan who has built a transmedial storyworld around delicious recipes, healthy nutrition, and her own brand. One of the most prominent is Tracye McQuirter, whose website, *By Any Greens Necessary*, answers not only questions about going vegan along with providing meal plans and nutrition tips, but also offers a free "21-Day-Vegan Fresh Start Guide." Like A. Breeze Harper, McQuirter was inspired to try out a plant-based diet by the teachings of Dick Gregory, whom she heard speak at an event at the University of Massachusetts in 1987, when she was a graduate student. She recalls how, on that day, "Gregory flipped the script. Instead of talking about the *state* of black America, he talked about the *plate* of black America – and how poorly black folks eat" (2010, loc 26). Worse still, he "graphically trace[d] the path of a hamburger from a cow on a factory farm to a fast-food restaurant to a heart attack" (loc 81). Shocked and impressed, McQuirter started on a path that led her to convince both her mother and her sister Marya to go vegetarian, then vegan with her. Together with Marya, she formed an organization called Vegan Versions and, in 1997, launched "the very first website by and for Black vegans and one of *the* first vegan websites" (Mercy for Animals Interview). As the technical capacities of the internet developed, the sisters created the first online magazine covering all aspects of veganism. By now, McQuirter is a trained nutritionist and a frequent public speaker who has published three books that combine extensive nutritional advice with information on animal and human rights, beautiful food photography, and a great variety of recipes.

Harper has noted that "the definite difference between McQuirter's representation of animal rights and veganism" in her book *By Any Greens Necessary* (2010) and that of more mainstream authors of vegan cookbooks, is that, as a Black woman, "McQuirter is able to speak simultaneously from race-conscious and animal-conscious approaches to veganism" (Harper 2012, 170). And indeed, in addition to relating her personal journey to veganism, McQuirter also digs into Black foodways and history. "Most of us are only a generation or two removed from the South," she writes in the book, "and not that many more generations removed from West Africa, where our forebears ate organic fruits, vegetables, and legumes daily that they plucked fresh from the fields of their own farms" (2010, loc 219). However, Harper also makes clear the limitations of McQuirter's cookbook in terms of food justice, complaining that "for someone who spoke of their race-class consciousness around food access at the beginning," McQuirter shows surprisingly little awareness of how difficult it is to get the necessary ingredients in the middle of a food desert. "Perhaps," she suggests caustically, "if McQuirter were to update her edition of the book, she could include a section guiding African American women on how to engage in food justice activism to get to the point where they can access what is on McQuirter's vegan food list" (2012, 171). The reason for the glaring omission regarding access, Harper suspects, might be that the book's target audience is Black women in a similar socio-economic situation as McQuirter's. Arguably, this class-consciousness is also expressed in the fact that no free recipes are available on the By All Greens Necessary website.

A more easily accessible approach to transmedial storytelling is demonstrated by Black vegan food bloggers such as Jenné Claiborne, who features hundreds of plant-based recipes on her *Sweet Potato Soul* blog, along with hundreds of cooking videos on her YouTube channel, TikTok, and Instagram. As the name of the blog suggests, Claiborne specializes in veganizing Soul Food and thus providing a plant-based alternative for those who want to hold on to the tastes and culinary desires of their youth and community without consuming animals products. In the introduction of her cookbook, also entitled *Sweet Potato Soul*, Claiborne writes that she has "grown accustomed to being asked if it's difficult to be a vegan from the South," and that she tells people "how much [she] adore[s] eating Southern food and how practical it is to make our staples totally vegan" (2020, 7). Soul Food and veganism, she makes clear, are easy to square if you know how. Claiborne provides this know-how across her media channels, taking advantage of each medium's affordances (Jenkins 2006). Her blog is easily searchable and constantly updated with new recipes that come with detailed instructions and carefully lit images of the complete dish. Unlike some other food bloggers, she does not provide step-by-step images because she can refer to her (by now) professionally produced videos, which combine virtual front-cooking with lighthearted anecdotes.

Like many vegan food bloggers and vloggers, Claiborne thus contributes to the increasingly widespread phenomenon of *vegan food porn*, which owes its popularity to the intensely positive emotions it evokes.[34] In her study on the popularization of veganism through food blogs in France, Ophélie Véron states that early vegan food bloggers intended to provide like-minded people with information that at the time was difficult to get," but that there has been a shift toward also "highlighting the culinary delights offered by the vegan cuisine and presenting it as a healthy and delicious alternative to meat-based food" (2016, 290). Almost without exception, such culinary delights are accompanied by "pornographic" food photography. In a 2015 article, entitled "What 'Food Porn' Does to the Brain," the journalist Cari Romm relates the popularity of attractively depicted food items to psychologist Deirdre Barrett's research on supernormal stimuli and her insight that "exaggerated imitation can cause a stronger pull than the real thing" (Barrett 3). Food porn, argues Romm, "is defined in part by the senses [in] that it is a visual experience

---

[34] The alluring depiction of food is sometimes referred to as "food porn" because of what some consider a structural similarity to the psychological mechanisms of sexual pornography.

of something that other people can smell and taste" (2015). While that is true, neuroscientist Vittorio Gallese explains that "vision is far more complex than the mere activation of the visual part of the brain" (2016, 4). Because vision is "multimodal," it allows us to simulate on the imaginary level several other sensual impressions, among them smell, taste, and texture. "Sight is critical in eating," writes food designer Barb Stuckey (2012, 2), even when the food is physically present. In the case of food porn, the supernormal stimulus of a carefully arranged and lit dish can be more engaging than the actual stimulus. Just looking at pictures of food can cause an uptick in ghrelin, a hormone that causes hunger (Schüssler et al. 2012). This is why Véron suggests that food blogs can contribute to the recognition that vegan food is not only healthy and ethical, but also attractive and desirable, as in the case of Claiborne's veganized Soul Food.

The difference between her and more mainstream vegan food bloggers – to echo Harper's earlier comment – is that as a Black woman Claiborne speaks simultaneously from race-conscious and animal-conscious approaches to veganism, although she does not foreground the former nearly as much as McQuirter does and rarely makes explicit references to food justice or the fact that some followers might have limited access to the necessary ingredients. This eschewing of the political dimensions of veganism is not unusual among more mainstream vegan vloggers. Daniela Pirani and Ella Fegitz observe that "what characterizes the recent popularity of [white veganism] is the move away from ethical and political motivations" (2019, 69). Even though Claiborne is Black, her blogging and vlogging are part of a larger trend that frames plant-based food as a tool to build a beautiful and healthy body and mind – and which displaces social and environmental responsibility, food justice, and animal welfare as secondary concerns. Regardless, the fact that most of Claiborne's recipes and videos are free means that they enable a different form of *access* – access to knowledge about vegan Soul Food and how to prepare it.

Jennifer Lofgren has noted that "while cookbooks and other forms of food-related media are well established as a means for recipes to be communicated, recipes have a longer history of being shared between individuals, that is, within families and communities" and that "blogging, and specifically food blogging, has emerged as a … viable way for people to share information about food in a non-professional capacity" (2013). This is true, and, as Véron has demonstrated, such information sharing is of great importance for vegan communities. Yet it is also true that successful bloggers and vloggers tend to expand and professionalize their work across multiple platforms as they create their own brands. Brown and McQuirter are cases in point, and so is Claiborne. In a 2022 video on her YouTube channel, she announced that while her brand is still strong and "her business is growing" along with her team and her platforms, she will do "YouTube more in a seasonal fashion" because producing a long YouTube video is so much more work and time-consuming "than doing the same thing for TikTok and Instagram, which are short-form videos" (Claiborne 2022). We see the same degree of professionalization also in Bryant Terry's work, to which I will now turn, but he has gone farther in developing his transmedial food storyworld, and he is also much more overtly invested in political issues around food justice.

Narrating from the Visceral to the Cerebral and the Political: Bryant Terry

Aside from his TEDMED talk, Terry has used his narrative agency to reframe the story of Black food and agricultural traditions in countless videos, along with five cookbooks. He has also created a "values-driven creative agency," Zenmi, which is "BIPOC focused," and dedicated to "authentic storytelling." Reading just one of Terry's cookbooks is meant to be a multimedia experience as he includes not only photographs but also sheet music, visual art, and "soundtracks" the reader might want to listen to while cooking and eating his dishes.[35] In her Foreword to *Afro-Vegan*, Jessica Harris writes that Terry's recipes made her recall "the first tastes of dishes sampled on the African continent that reminded me of those eaten in my grandmothers' kitchens" (2014, 8), while reading his proposed soundtrack, she "heard the background music of [her] own journey" (8). Reading the names of the Black writers and artists also mentioned in the book led her to "mentally pour ... rum on the ground for the repose of those friends who are gathered at the table in the sky" (8). It is this deliberate cueing of embodied simulation (Gallese 2016) and the resulting multisensory connection to the creative and sensual dimensions of a past that needs to be carefully recovered and reinterpreted that is typical for Terry's transmedial vegan food storyworld.

The fact that Harris reports in her Foreword that she was smiling as she read through the pages of *Afro-Vegan*, because it was "in many ways it is a trip down memory lane" (2014, 8) is in line with the Terry's expressed goals as both a chef and a self-described "radial food justice activist." Like McQuirter and Levya, he traces Black foodways back to pre-colonial times to displace the meat-centeredness of what Harper calls "postindustrialized Soul Food practices"

---

[35] There are competing definitions of inter-, multi-, and transmediality. In my context, the term "multimediality" refers to "the occurrence where there are many media in one and the same object" (Kattenbelt 2009, 20).

(2010, xix). In the interview with Omowale Adewale featured in the *Brotha Vegan* anthology, Terry explains that a large part of his work "is about helping my people remember that our traditional diets are replete with nutrient-dense dark-green leafy vegetables, protein-rich legumes, vitamin-packed fruits, and the like" (Adewale 2021, 26). His motivation to write *Afro-Vegan*, along with his other cookbooks, was "to move Afro-diasporic food from the margins closer to the center of our collective culinary consciousness and to put its ingredients, cooking techniques, and flavor profiles into wider circulation" (2014, 11). Arguably, this motivation is shared by all the Black vegan cookbook authors, food vloggers, and filmmakers I have discussed so far.

However, Terry's transmedial project does not stop at the re-centering of Afro-diasporic food, or even refreshing people's memories about the long and influential tradition of African farming techniques – a passion he shares with Malik Yakini and Leah Penniman. Like the two farmer-activists, he also connects these ancient techniques to discourses around environmental and food justice, but he makes all of it palatable via the evocation of tasty vegan dishes. "Through cookbook writing" he explains in *Afro-Vegan*, "I strive to open the door for more people to have pleasurable experiences with wholesome, fresh food, which I believe is a revolutionary first step toward food justice" (223). This is why the book, as Marilisa Navarro has put it, is a case study "in anti-racist practice" (2021, 283) that puts much "emphasis on the nutritional elements" of the recipes (285), but never forgets to foreground their delicious-ness. To use Terry's mantra once again, which he repeats across all his cook-books: he starts "*with the visceral to ignite the cerebral and end with the political*" (2014, 223; emphasis in original). Assisted by generously lit vegan food porn, his books and cooking videos present Afro-diasporic dishes and encourage readers and viewers to try them out themselves – something which they may or may not do – while also educating them about the health benefits of plant-based food and the need to change the Black diet as part of a larger fight for racial justice, which includes access to fresh and culturally appropriate ingredients.[36]

A good example of how this process can work in the realm of visual narrative is a thirty-minute video entitled "Sustenance and Liberation" (2023) produced by Terry's Zenmi agency, in which he appears together with Black Feast founder Salimatu Amabebe.[37] The video starts out with a horizontal split screen

---

[36] In the *Sustenance and Liberation* video, Terry acknowledges that he has been criticized for the complexity of his recipes but insists that he wants people to have "the skills to make things from scratch."

[37] Black Feast is a culinary event originating in Portland, OR that celebrates Black artists and writers through food.

and some serious food porn as the two chefs create one vegan dish each. They are working in two kitchens, connected on the auditory level by the underlying spiritual song "Glory, Glory." As soon as the two settings and protagonists are visually established, the video cuts to extreme close-ups of the produce the chefs are working with – kale, bell peppers, tomatoes, basil, onions – showing their hands and knives peeling, slicing, and chopping, the produce rendered in bright, luscious colors. Crosscutting between the two sets shows the cooking process, each shot revealing a new step of boiling, frying, stirring, and seasoning. The ninety-second sequence ends with close-ups of the completed dishes before cutting to a medium shot that shows a rectangular table placed in a yard filled with eucalyptus trees and daffodils. It is covered by a blue-and-white tablecloth and the dishes, arranged with a vase of tulips and a bottle of chilly oil. At the table ends, the two chefs sit in front of their plates, ready for a conversation that starts with the food they prepared for each other and then moves on to the work they do, using cooking as a community-building tool to work against food injustice and reacquaint Black people with the traditions of the African diaspora.

Keeping Terry's mantra in mind, it is easy to see how the video goes from the visceral (the mouthwatering close-ups showing the ingredients and preparation of the food) to the cerebral (the chefs talking about how they made it and how that is connected to the traditions of the African diaspora) and ends at the political (the chefs talking about their activist work and the challenges ahead). Evoking the sensory dimensions of delicious vegan food either visually or verbally in a way that enables embodied simulation is one of Terry's strengths as a chef, cookbook author, and transmedial food justice activist. In the "Sustenance and Liberation" video, Amabebe tells him: "Hearing you talk about a dish is like ASMR, it's very soothing." ASMR is the acronym for *autonomous sensory meridian response*, a term used to describe "a tingling, static-like, or goosebumps sensation in response to specific triggering audio or visual stimuli .... When experiencing ASMR sensations, some people report pleasant feelings of relaxation, calm, sleepiness or well-being" (*Nebraska Medicine* 2022). A study by psychologists Nicole Woods and Julie Turner-Cobb also shows that "ASMR appears to play an important role in promoting health and mental wellbeing" (2023, 2337), which might be an important factor also in the popularity of Tabitha Brown's feel-good cooking videos. However, unlike Brown, Terry does not want the reception of his Soul Food work to stop at this comfortable bodily, visceral level. Rather, he wants it to "ignite the cerebral" (2009, 318) and thus related cognitive processes – aka critical thinking – about the larger *political* repercussions of the vegan sustenance that promotes such good feelings and well-being, and how it is related to questions of justice.

By now, there are countless such entry points into Bryant Terry's transmedia storyworld. People can start with his website, cookbooks, TED talk, artwork, Instagram, or any of the other videos and television appearances, or they can book a cooking class with him. His most recent book, *Black Food* (2021), is a partial departure in that it is an anthology featuring the recipes, essays, and artwork of more than 100 contributors throughout the Black diaspora – including Leah Penniman and Jenné Claiborne – and that it is one of two books that include not only vegan but also vegetarian and several meat- or fish-based recipes. In the "Sustenance and Liberation" video, Terry explains that the book was created during the Covid pandemic as a "gift to the movement," distributing narrative agency among other Black chefs, artists, and activists, and that this is yet another mediated mode of food justice activism. Most recently, he has become the editor of 4 Color, an imprint of Ten Speed Press/Penguin Random House, which will "craft visually stunning nonfiction books that inspire readers and give rise to a more beautiful, healthy, just, and sustainable world." As in the case of Brown and the other authors whose work I have discussed here, the distinction between commerce and activism is not always clear-cut because it has become symbiotic.

While I have treated them in separate parts, and proponents of community gardening projects are not necessarily promoting vegan diets, it should not come as a surprise that vegan food justice activists such as Terry embrace gardening as a practical way to access fresh produce in the middle of food deserts and reconnect with Black agricultural traditions. The fact that Penniman contributes a recipe she learned from her grandmother to Terry's *Black Food* anthology is a gesture to that connection, and there is an entire series of videos on the YouTube channel *Nourish Life* in which Terry speaks about the vital importance of urban farming for the food justice struggle of the Black community.[38] Moreover, he has also made his personal backyard gardening part of his storyworld. In a #HowIGotHere video produced by LinkedIn News, he walks toward the vegetable beds outside his house while the audio track continues from the previous scene, which showed him cooking.[39] "If I were to trace my interest in food," he says, "I think I would go back to my childhood in Memphis, Tennessee. Being in my grandmother's kitchen ... I witness[ed] her making food from scratch almost every day that she grew in her own backyard garden. That agrarian knowledge, that desire to connect with food, those were the things transmitted to me." No matter which entry point, then, audiences are

---

[38] See, for example, the episode "Bryant Terry: Urban Farms" of *Nourish: Food and Community* from 2010: www.youtube.com/watch?v=CCRFSAxGeJs.

[39] The video is available at www.youtube.com/watch?v=cUMO2OdJIws.

always invited to engage with Terry's core narrative about food sovereignty, food justice, and the culinary and emotional value of the Black diaspora.

Conclusion

The vegan reimagining of Soul Food as a community-building tool and a mode of cultural resilience seems to have made inroads in the communities it wants to reach. A 2021 article by Bridget Kuehn reports that vegan diets that are culturally aligned with traditional Soul Food have been gaining popularity among Black individuals and that positive health effects have been measured in the NEW Soul Study program. Citing a nurse collaborating on the study, Kuehn reports that participants in the program "are reassured when they learn that they can continue to eat traditional dishes like collard greens or candied yams but with some healthier substitutions" (2021). While it is difficult to attribute such changes directly to the transmedial work of the Black nutritionists, activist chefs, and food bloggers I have discussed here, they show that it is possible to shift people's eating habits toward healthy, culturally appropriate food. Aph Ko has argued that we should resist reducing veganism to a way of eating or lifestyle and understand that, like other social movements, it is about "powerful conversations for change" (2019, 8) The focus on creating delicious vegan food in the narratives I have discussed here is nevertheless a valuable corrective to the larger food justice movement's primary concern with "oppression and inequity in the food system" in which food only "demarcates the focus of struggle" (Sbicca 2018, loc 115). Much as the environment itself should be a concern in environmental justice struggles, food as nourishment and pleasure should be a focus of food justice struggles, not only because access to produce alone will not make people any healthier, but also because the path from the visceral to the cerebral ultimately becomes an important road to political engagement. "What we choose to eat is not merely a logical decision; it is a product of our identity, spirituality, and affective relationships within our communities," writes Christopher Carter, "The story of soul food must remain a story of resistance, resilience, community, and empowerment" (2021).

If in 2018, Julia Turshen still had reason to complain about the lack of diversity among the authors of vegan cookbooks, this has changed dramatically in recent years. While I have focused here on narratives about Black vegan food, similar efforts have emerged also from other communities of color in the U.S. Examples include food blogs by Richa Hingl, Eva Agha, and Joanne Molinaro, and cookbooks such as *Provecho* by Edgar Castrejón (2021) and Luz Calvo and Catriona Rueda's *Decolonize Your Diet* (2015), which combines recipes for vegan Mesoamerican food with an attention to food justice struggles. Navarro, who discusses the latter book together with Terry's *Afro-Vegan,* lauds it for communicating "messages of resistance to legacies of racism, violence, and injustice by referencing histories of struggle and survival" (2021, 289) without forgetting the live-giving quality and seductiveness of delicious food. If farming is an inherently hopeful practice even in adverse circumstances, then creating and sharing recipes for plant-based and culturally appropriate dishes is another one. As the vegan chef Fred "Doc" Beasley II puts it in his contribution to *Brotha Vegan*, among the most important relationships one develops are those with "the young people you teach. I love working with them and seeing that flash of insight and curiosity; I love seeing that connection being restored and filled with hope" (2021, 169). Calvo and Esquibel similarly "hope that as we energize our bodies and spirits with wholesome food, we also energize ourselves to continue to struggle for decolonization and food justice" (2015, 17). In recent years, the connection between organic community farming and veganism as modes of resistance to colonizing food systems has also found expression in trends toward *veganic* farming – the organic production of food with no or minimal animal inputs – as practiced, for example, by the Black food justice activist Eugene Cook in Atlanta who promotes veganic growing methods in urban areas through the Grow Where You Are Collective.[40] It is my hope that these joint movements will continue and thrive.

Afterword: Toward Real Food Utopias

Regardless of whether they play out on the local, national, or global level, food justice narratives are inextricably intertwined with planetary concerns. In part due to spatial constraints, I have focused on American food justice narratives in this Element, but there are an infinite number of other stories told about food justice struggles in the interests of both human and nonhuman animals around the world. *Growing Hope* has grown out of my own hope that engaging with (vegan) food justice narratives can show those of us who are wondering how we can still mitigate and adapt to our ongoing climate emergency some possible paths forward. Contrary to common expectations, empirical studies have shown that urban agriculture will not necessarily attract capital, leading to displacement and gentrification. Rather, "its greatest potential is in social enterprise, supplementing incomes, developing human and social capital and promoting food security" (Vitiello & Wolf-Powers 2014, 508). Urban community gardening and grassroots farming practices are thus an important step toward ensuring food security and justice while also greening cities and thereby contributing to

---

[40] More information on the collective is available at www.growwhereyouare.farm. For more information on veganic farming more generally, see Jimmy Videle's *The Veganic Grower's Handbook* (2022).

making them more livable and resilient to climatic changes (De Zeeuw 2011). While the way we grow and eat our food is not the only factor affecting the climate and a host of other environmental crises, it is a substantial one. Not only can we choose to at least partially opt out of the industrial food system and eat healthier, less wasteful, and more ethical, plant-based diets, but we can also support our own or other communities in their fight for food justice.

However, it is not only individual humans and communities who are at risk because of the industrial agricultural complex's largely invisible ways of producing food, but nonhuman animals, ecosystems, and the health of the entire planet are also at stake. Eliza Barcley warns in her introductory note for the *New York Times's* "What to Eat on a Burning Planet" series that although "the organic and plant-based food movements have helped shift production and consumption patterns ever so slightly, we remain dependent on a largely unsustainable food system that's destroying precious resources as it races to feed the world" (2024). Narratives about community gardening and vegan food justice promote ways of being in the world that can improve physical and emotional health, and they have the potential to not only address current inequities on the local, national, and global levels, but also help reduce the weight of humanity's outsized ecological footprint on the planet, something we urgently need. In *Panik Now?* (2024, xi), Ira Allen postulates that rather than hoping that the carbon, capitalist, colonial world we are currently inhabiting can somehow be saved, we should start "panicking wisely" and "in time," so that we might come up with "new visions of a global humanity in deep relation with the more-than-human world." In this logic, accepting our current demise is the first step toward growing *radical* hope for genuine change.

The path I have chosen here, from urban community gardening to vegan food justice and from documentary filmmaking to more transmedial forms of engagement, is not meant to devalue the former. While I respect and support communities' claims to their right of self-representation, and while I see great advantages in flexible storytelling modes that can continue for long time periods across a variety of media channels, I do not necessarily think that there is anything wrong with making a film about, and in collaboration with, affected communities. In *Affective Ecologies*, I called this the "outsider perspective" to injustice (2017, 85), which is different from, but not necessarily less valuable than the "insider perspective" provided by community members, especially if the community has a say in the representation of their story, as it is the case for all the documentaries I have discussed here. Several of the examples I have provided demonstrate that it can be a both/and rather than either/or decision, since seasoned activists collaborate with photographers, videographers, and filmmakers and make use of additional professional expertise to create one more entry point into their vast nonfiction storyworlds and thus one more way for people to become engaged and supportive of their struggles for food justice.

This leaves open at least one more question, one that concerns narrative impact. In his interview with David Poland ahead of the 2010 Academy Awards ceremony, Scott Hamilton Kennedy emphasized that what matters most to him as a filmmaker is that the story he tells about the tragic loss of the South Central Farm is *engaging*. An engaged filmmaker himself, Kennedy is invested in the social justice narratives that some of his films portray, but he also feels a need to "keep people's heads from hitting the desk" out of boredom (Poland 2010) – a sure sign of disengagement. Food justice activists such as Leah Penniman and Bryant Terry have spoken of the central importance of engagement to their activist community work, with the difference that it offers many more possibilities for their audiences to get directly involved, be it physically, financially, or politically. As I have argued we need both modes of engagement and they are not mutually exclusive, but rather complementary. And yet, ecocritical media scholars, filmmakers, and activists alike need to develop a better understanding of *how* different media modes engage audiences and what works "better" in terms of a narrative's aim. Food justice activists can gauge the impact of their campaigns by the number of people who join and show up or by the donations and support they receive, and that is what matters most in the end. However, they would nevertheless profit from a better understanding of the impact of their chosen narrative strategies and media channels.

For these reasons, I still see the need for developing more structured ways of measuring not only reception but also resulting actions. Together with colleagues in the Netherlands and Germany, I have begun tackling some of these important questions in relation to documentary films with sustainability themes, but we are only at the beginning of studying reception in conjunction with close analysis of the narratives themselves, an approach that falls under the broader umbrella of empirical ecocriticism (Schneider-Mayerson et al. 2023). Some of this research could be done in collaboration with activists, NGOs, and "impact producers" in the film and media industry as well as the communities they hope to engage with their narratives.[41] Such collaborative research is not only interdisciplinary but also *transdisciplinary* in the European tradition of the term, which "includes both cross-disciplinarity and stakeholder involvement"

---

[41] According to the *Impact Field Guide* (2020), impact producers are "deliberate about who needs to see a film, what audiences need to do, and what partnerships, tools and resources are needed to reach the desired goals of the campaign."

(Bennich et al. 2022) to develop "approaches that connect scholars to society and research to action" (Knapp et al. 2019). Although such approaches have already been used successfully in other disciplines, I do not mean to suggest that transdisciplinary research on food justice or other environmental narratives is easy to develop or carry out. But my hope is that, given the interlocking environmental crises we are facing and the long histories of exploitation and inequity they continue to exacerbate, we will find ways to not only tell stories that represent and intervene in this development, but also modes of research that help us understand and respond to their impact.

References

Abbot, Mathew. 2019. "*Grey Gardens* and the Problem of Objectivity." *Projections: The Journal for Movies and Mind* 13(2): 108–122.

Adams, Carol J. 1990. *The Sexual Politics of Meat: A Feminist-Vegetarian Critical Theory*. London: Continuum.

———. 2017. Afterword. In *Aphro-ism: Essays on Pop Culture, Feminism, and Black Veganism from Two Sisters*, edited by Aph Ko and Syl Ko, 139–148. New York: Lantern Books.

Adewale, Omawale. 2021. "Brotherhood: An Interview with Bryant Terry." In *Brotha Vegan: Black Men Speak on Food, Identity, Health, and Society*, edited by Omawale Adewale, 26–30. New York: Lantern.

Agyeman, Julian, and Jesse McEntee. 2014. "Moving the Field of Food Justice Forward Through the Lens of Urban Political Ecology." *Geography Compass* 8(3): 211–220.

Aksu, Ali. 2023. "How the Film Industry Can Shift Toward Impact-Oriented Storytelling." *Forbes* (July 13). www.forbes.com/sites/forbesbusiness council/2023/07/13/how-the-film-industry-can-shift-toward-impact-oriented-storytelling/.

Alkon, Alison Hope, and Julian Agyeman, eds. 2011. *Cultivating Food Justice: Race, Class, and Sustainability*. Cambridge, MA: MIT Press.

Alkon, Allison Hope, and Josh Cadji. 2020. "Sowing Seeds of Displacement: Gentrification and Food Justice in Oakland, CA." *International Journal of Urban and Regional Research* 44(1): 108–123.

Alkon, Allison Hope, and Kari Marie Norgaard. 2009. "Breaking the food chains: An Investigation of Food Justice Activism." *Sociological Inquiry* 79(3): 289–305.

Allen, Ira J. 2024. *Panik Now? Tools for Humanizing*. Knoxville: University of Tennessee Press.

Bailey, Allison. 2018. "On Anger, Silence and Epistemic Injustice." *Royal Institute of Philosophy Supplement* 84: 93–115.

Barclay, Eliza. 2024. "What to Eat on a Burning Planet." *New York Times Opinion* (July 29). www.nytimes.com/2024/07/29/opinion/what-to-eat-on-a-burning-planet.html.

Barrett, Deirdre. 2010. *Supernormal Stimuli: How Primal Urges Overran Their Evolutionary Purpose*. New York: Norton.

Bennich, Therese, Giorgos Maneas, Sofia Maniatakou, Luigi Piemontese, Christina Schaffer, Marie Schellens and Carl Österlin. 2022. "Transdisciplinary

Research for Sustainability: Scoping for Project Potential." *International Social Science Journal* 72(246): 1087–1104.

Bergesen, Albert, and Max Herman. 1998. "Immigration, Race, and Riot: The 1992 Los Angeles Uprising." *American Sociological Review* 63(1): 39–54.

Besaw, Bridget, dir. 2024. *Rooted*. Documentary film.

Bittman, Mark. 2022. *Animal, Vegetable, Junk*. New York: HarperCollins.

Bowie, Richard. 2020. "Black Wellness Matters: How Vegan TikTok Star Tabitha Brown is Healing Her Community." *VegNews* (May 31). https://vegnews .com/2020/5/black-wellness-matters-how-vegan-tiktok-star-tabitha-brown- is-healing-her-community.

Bringle, Robert G., Ashley Hedgepath, and Elizabeth Wall. 2018. "'I Am So Angry I Could ... Help!': The Nature of Empathic Anger." *International Journal of Research on Service-Learning and Community Engagement* 6(1): Article 3.

Brooker, Jena. 2023. "Hantz Tree Farm Falls Short on Solving East Side Blight." *Bridge Detroit* (January 26). www.bridgedetroit.com/john- hantz-tree-farm-detroit-east-side-blight/.

Brown, Sandy, and Christy Getz. 2011. "Farmworker Food Insecurity and the Production of Hunger in California." In *Cultivating Food Justice: Race, Class, and Sustainability*, edited by Alison Hope Alkon and Julian Agyeman, 121–145. Cambridge, MA: MIT Press.

Braun, Virginia and Sophie Carruthers. 2020. "Working at Self and Wellness: A Critical Analysis of Vegan Vlogs." In *Digital Food Cultures*, edited by Deborah Lupton and Zeena Feldman, 82–96. New York: Routledge.

Brown, Tabhita. "I Am Tabitha Brown." www.iamtabithabrown.com/.

2021. *Feeding the Soul*. New York: William Morrow.

Bullard, Robert D. 1990. *Dumping in Dixie: Race, Class, and Environmental Quality*. Boulder: Westview.

Caldwell, Erin M., M. Miller Kobayashi, W. M. DuBow, and S. M. Wytinck. 2008. "Perceived Access to Fruits and Vegetables Associated with Increased Consumption." *Public Health Nutrition* 12(10): 1743–1750. https://doi.org/10.1017/S1368980008004308.

Calvo, Luz, and Catriona Rueda. 2015. *Decolonize Your Diet*. Vancouver: Arsenal Pulp Press.

Campbell, Hugh. 2015. "Spurlock's Vomit and Visible Food Utopias." In *Food Utopias: Reimagining Citizenship, Ethics and Community*, edited by Paul V. Stock, Michael Carolan, and Christopher Rosin, 195–215. New York: Routledge.

Cano-Verdugo, Guillermo, Brianda Daniela Flores-García, Georgina Mayela Núñez-Rocha, María Natividad Ávila-Ortíz, and María Argelia Akemi Nakagoshi-Cepeda. 2024. "Impact of Urban Farming on Health: a

Systematic Review." *Journal of Public Health*. fdae056. https://doi.org/10.1093/pubmed/fdae056.

Carolan, Michael. 2015. "Re-Wilding Food Systems: Visceralities, Utopias, Pragmatism, and Practice." In *Food Utopias: An Invitation to a Food Dialogue*, edited by Paul V. Stock, Christopher Rosin, and Michael Carolan, 126–139. New York: Routledge.

Carruth, Allison. 2013. *Global Appetites: American Power and the Literature of Food*. Cambridge: Cambridge University Press.

Carter, Christopher. 2021. *The Spirit of Soul Food: Race, Faith, and Food Justice*. Urbana-Champaign: University of Illinois Press.

Catsoulis, Jeannette. 2009. "The Seeds of a Community Conflict." *New York Times* (May 7). www.nytimes.com/2009/05/08/movies/08gard.html.

    2014. "The Seeds of an Urban Protest." *New York Times* (November 14). www.nytimes.com/2014/11/14/movies/occupy-the-farm-a-documentary-by-todd-darling.html.

Claiborne, Jenné. 2018. *Sweet Potato Soul*. New York: Harmony.

    2022. "Time to Say Goodbye." *SweetPotatoSoul YouTube Channel*. https://www.youtube.com/watch?v=CjwO_El6XC4.

Clendenning, Jessica, Wolfram H. Dressler, and Carol Richards. 2015. "Food Justice or Food Sovereignty? Understanding the Rise of Urban Food Movements in the USA." *Agriculture And Human Values* 33(1): 165–77. https://doi.org/10.1007/s10460-015-9625-8.

Colasanti, Kathryn J. A., Michael W. Hamm, and Charlotte M. Litjens. 2012. "The City as an 'Agricultural Powerhouse'? Perspectives on Expanding Urban Agriculture from Detroit, Michigan." *Urban Geography* 33(3): 348–369.

Danielle, Melissa. 2009. "Nutrition Liberation: Plant-based Diets as a Tool for Healing, Resistance, and Self-Reliance." In *Sistah Vegan: Black Female Vegans Speak on Food, Identity, Health, and Society*, edited by A. Breeze Harper, 47–52. New York: Lantern.

Darling, Todd, dir. 2014. *Occupy the Farm*. Ignite Channel.

Dibsdall, L. A., Nigel Lambert, R. F. Bobbin, and Lynn Jayne Frewe. 2003. "Low-income Consumers' Attitudes and Behaviour towards Access, Availability and Motivation to Eat Fruit and Vegetables." *Public Health Nutrition* 6(2): 159–168.

Discussion Carsey-Wolf Center. 2015. "Occupy the Farm." Discussion with Todd Darling and Ashoka Finley. Carsey-Wolf Center (April 14). https://www.carseywolf.ucsb.edu/pollock-events/occupy-the-farm/.

Dowmunt, Tony. 2013. "Autobiographical Documentary—the 'Seer and the Seen.'" *Studies in Documentary Film* 7(3): 263–277.

Drew, Ain. 2010. "Bein a Sistah at PETA." In *Sistah Vegan: Black Female Vegans Speak on Food, Identity, Health, and Society*, edited by A. Breeze Harper, 61–64. New York: Lantern.

Dubowitz, Tamara, Shannon N. Zenk, Bonnie Ghosh-Dastidar et al. 2015. "Healthy Food Access for Urban Food Desert Residents: Examination of the Food Environment, Food Purchasing Practices, Diet and BMI." *Public Health Nutrition* 18, 2220–2230.

Durham, Delicia. 2010. "One Being Black and Vegan." In *Sistah Vegan: Black Female Vegans Speak on Food, Identity, Health, and Society*, edited by A. Breeze Harper, 43–46. New York: Lantern.

Eitzen, Dirk. 2005. "Documentary's Peculiar Appeals." In *Moving Image Theory*, edited by Joseph D. Anderson and Barbara Fisher Anderson, 183–199. Carbondale: Southern Illinois University Press.

Emmett, Robert S. 2016. *Cultivating Environmental Justice: A Literary History of U.S. Garden Writing*. Amherst & Boston: University of Massachusetts Press.

Enck-Wanzer, Darrel. 2011. "Race, Coloniality, and Geo-Body Politics: *The Garden* as Latin@ Vernacular Discourse." *Environmental Communication* 5(3): 363–371.

Fiskio, Janet. 2012. "Unsettling Ecocriticism: Rethinking Agrarianism, Place, and Citizenship." *American Literature* 84(2): 301–325.

Forgrieve, Janet. 2018. "The Growing Acceptance of Veganism." *Forbes*. www.forbes.com/sites/janetforgrieve/2018/11/02/picturing-a-kindler-gentler-world-vegan-month/.

Francis, Dania V., Darrick Hamilton, Thomas Mitchell, Nathan A. Rosenberg, and Bryce Wilson Stucki. 2022. "Black Land Loss: 1920–1997." *AEA Papers and Proceedings* 112: 38–42.

French, Lisa. 2019. "Women Documentary Filmmakers as Transnational 'Advocate Change Agents.'" *Inter-disciplina* 7(17): 15–29. https://doi.org/10.22201/ceiich.24485705e.2019.17.67536.

Gallese, Vittorio. 2016. "Bodily Framing." In *Experience: Culture, Cognition and the Common Sense*, edited by Caroline Jones, David Mather, and Rebecca Uchill, 1–15. Cambridge, MA: MIT Press.

Gilson, Erinn, and Sarah Kenehan, eds. 2018. *Food, Environment, and Climate Change: Justice at the Intersections*. New York: Rowman & Littlefield.

Giraud, Eva Haifa. 2021. *Veganism*. London: Bloomsbury.

Glennie, Charlotte, and Alison Hope Alkon. 2018. "Food Justice: Cultivating the Field." *Environmental Research Letters* 13: 073003.

Glowa, Michelle. 2017. "Urban Agriculture, Food justice and Neoliberal Urbanization: Rebuilding the Institution of Property." In *The New Food*

Activism, edited by Alison Alkon and Julie Guthman, 232–255. Berkeley: University of California Press.

Gregory, Peter J., John S. I. Ingram, and Michael Brklacich. 2005. "Climate Change and Food Security." *Philosophical Transactions of the Royal Society B* 360: 2139–2148. https://doi.org/10.1098/rstb.2005.1745.

Grotto, David, and Elsa Zied. 2010. "The Standard American Diet and Its Relationship to the Health Status of Americans." *Nutrition in Clinical Practice* 25(6): 603–612.

Hancox, Donna. 2021. "Transmedia Storytelling and Activism." *The Writing Platform* (December 6). https://thewritingplatform.com/2021/12/transme dia-storytelling-and-activism/.

Hardy, Ernest. 2014. "*Occupy the Farm* Remembers One of the Movement's Successes." *Village Voice* (September 12). www.villagevoice.com/ occupy-the-farm-remembers-one-of-the-movements-successes/.

Harper, A. Breeze, ed. 2010. *Sistah Vegan: Black Female Vegans Speak on Food, Identity, Health, and Society.* New York: Lantern.

Harper, A. Breeze. 2010b. "Race as a 'Feeble Matter'." *Journal for Critical Animal Studies* 8(3): 5–27.

2012. "Going Beyond the Normative White 'Post-Racial' Vegan Epistemology." In *Taking Food Public: Redefining Foodways in a Changing World*, edited by Psyche Williams-Forson and Carole Counihan, 155–174. New York: Routledge.

2017. Foreword. *Aphro-ism: Essays on Pop Culture, Feminism, and Black Veganism from Two Sisters* by Aph Ko and Syl Ko. New York: Lantern Books.

2021. Foreword. *Brotha Vegan: Black Men Speak on Food, Identity, Health, and Society*, edited by Omowale Adewale. New York: Lantern.

Harris, Jessica. 2014. Foreword. *Afro-Vegan: Farm-Fresh African, Caribbean, and Southern Flavors Remixed.* By Bryant Terry. Berkeley: Ten Speed Press.

Hasse, Andrew, dir. 2014. *Edible City.* Collective Eye Films.

Hawes, Jason K., Dimitrios Gounaridis, and Joshua P. Newell. 2022. "Does Urban Agriculture Lead to Gentrification?" *Landscape and Urban Planning* 225: 104447.

Heise, Ursula. 2020. "Afterword: Econarratology for the Future." In *Environment and Narrative: New Directions in Econarratology*, edited by Erin James and Eric Morel, 203–211. Columbus: Ohio State University Press.

Herman, David. 2009. "Narrative Ways of Worldmaking." In *Narratology in the Age of Cross-Disciplinary Narrative Research*, edited by Sandra Heinen & Roy Sommer, 71–86. Berlin: DeGruyter.

Hofmann, Martin. 2000. *Empathy and Moral Development: Implications for Caring and Justice*. Cambridge: Cambridge University Press.

Holloway, John. 2005. *Change the World Without Taking Power: The Meaning of Revolution Today*. London: Pluto Press.

Holmes, Jessica. 2021. "Vegan Studies and Food Studies." In *The Routledge Handbook of Vegan Studies*, edited by Laura White, 172–179. New York: Routledge.

Hughes, Helen. 2014. *Green Documentary: Environmental Documentary in the 21st Century*. Bristol: Intellect.

Imbibe & Inspire. 2012. "Interview #26 Mark MacInnis." www.youtube.com/watch?v=mTAYH06leIY.

Işıkman, Nihan Gider. 2018. "A Milestone in Film History: Smartphone Filmmaking." *International Journal of Culture and History* 4(4): 97–101.

Jenkins, Henry. 2006. *Convergence Culture: Where Old and New Media Collide*. New York: New York University Press.

Jones, pattrice. 2010. "Afterword: Liberation as Connection for the Decolonization of Desire." In *Sistah Vegan: Black Female Vegans Speak on Food, Identity, Health, and Society*, edited by A. Breeze Harper, 187–200. New York: Lantern.

Joseph A. Myers Center for Research on Native American Issues & Native American Student Development. 2021. *The University of California Land Grab: A Legacy of Profit from Indigenous Land—A Report of Key Learnings and Recommendations*. UC Berkeley.

Karpyn, Allison, Candace R. Young, Zachary Collier, and Karen Glanz. 2020. "Correlates of Healthy Eating in Urban Food Desert Communities." *International Journal of Environmental Research and Public Health* 17: 6305. https://doi.org/10.3390/ijerph17176305. www.mdpi.com/journal/ijerph.

Kattenbelt, Chiel. 2009. "Intermediality in Theatre and Performance: Definitions, Perceptions and Medial Relationships." *Cultura, Lenguaje Y Representación* 6: 19–29.

Kavada, Anastasia. 2015. "Creating the Collective: Social Media, the Occupy Movement and Its Constitution as a Collective Actor." *Information, Communication & Society* 18(8): 872–886.

Keleman, Adam. 2009. Review: *The Garden*. *Slant Magazine* (May 8) www.slantmagazine.com/film/the-garden/.

Kennedy, Scott Hamilton, dir. 2008. *The Garden*. Oscilloscope Pictures.

Kim, Claire Jean. 2011. "Moral Extensionism or Racist Exploitation? The Use of Holocaust and Slavery Analogies in the Animal Liberation Movement." *New Political Science* 33(3): 311–333.

Kim, Sue. 2014. *On Anger: Race, Cognition, Narrative*. Austin: University of Texas Press.

Klestil, Matthias, 2023. *Environmental Knowledge, Race, and African American Literature*. Basingstoke: Palgrave Macmillan.

Knapp, Corrine Nöel, Robin S. Reid, María E. Fernández-Giménez, Julia A. Klein and Kathleen A. Galvin. 2019. "Placing Transdisciplinarity in Context: A Review of Approaches to Connect Scholars, Society and Action." *Sustainability* 11(18): 4899.

Ko, Aph. 2019. *Racism as Zoological Witchcraft: A Guide to Getting Out*. New York: Lantern.

Ko, Aph, and Syl Ko. 2017. *Aphro-ism: Essays on Pop Culture, Feminism, and Black Veganism from Two Sisters*. New York: Lantern Books.

Kretzer, Andreas. 2021. "Beyond the Haze of Carnival Candles: Cinematic Space in Architectural Design Education." In *Handbook of Research on Methodologies for Design and Production Practices in Interior Architecture*, edited by Ervin Garip and S. Banu Garip, 21–43. Hershey: IGI Global.

Kuehn Bridget M. 2021. "Vegan Diets That Are Culturally Aligned with Traditional Soul Food Gain Popularity Among Black Individuals." *Circulation* 144: 393–394.

Kuipers, Dean. 2020. "Digging the Dirt on an L.A. Farm." *Alta* (April 23). www.altaonline.com/dispatches/a7718/dean-kuipers-los-angeles-farm/.

Lang, Cady. (2021, September 22). Tabitha Brown Is the Gentlest Person on the Internet. TIME. https://time.com/6100891/tabitha-brown-profile/.

Lear, Jonathan. 2006. *Radical Hope: Ethics in the Face of Cultural Devastation*. Cambridge, MA: Harvard University Press.

Levya, Jasmine, dir. 2019. *The Invisible Vegan*.

Lockwood, Alex. 2021. "Vegan Studies and Gender Studies." In *The Routledge Handbook of Vegan Studies*, edited by Laura White, 295–305. New York: Routledge.

Lofgren, Jennifer. 2013. "Food Blogging and Food-related Media Convergence." *M/C Journal* 16(3). https://doi.org/10.5204/mcj.638.

López, Antonio, Adrian Ivakhiv, Stephen Rust, et al., eds. 2023. *The Routledge Handbook of Ecomedia Studies*. New York: Routledge.

Lucertini, Giulia, and Gianmarco Di Giustino. 2021. "Urban and Peri-Urban Agriculture as a Tool for Food Security and Climate Change Mitigation and Adaptation: The Case of Mestre." *Sustainability* 13: 5999. https://doi.org/10.3390/su13115999.

MacInnis, Mark, dir. 2011. *Urban Roots*. Tree Media.

Malone, Melanie. 2022. "Seeking Justice, Eating toxics: Overlooked Contaminants in Urban Community Gardens." *Agriculture and Human Values* 39: 165–184.

Małecki, Wojciech, Piotr Sorokowski, Bogusław Pawłowski, and Marcin Cieński. 2019. *Human Minds and Animal Stories: How Narratives Make Us Care About Other Species.* New York and London: Routledge.

Mares, Teresa, and Devon Peña. 2010. "Urban Agriculture in the Making of Insurgent Spaces in Los Angeles and Seattle." In *Insurgent Public Space: Guerilla Urbanism and the Remaking of Contemporary Cities*, edited by Jeffrey Hou, 241–254. New York: Routledge.

Marris, Emma. 2011. *Rambunctious Garden: Saving Nature in a Post-Wild World.* London: Bloomsbury.

Mauch, Christof. 2019. *Slow Hope. Rethinking Ecologies of Crisis and Fear.* RCC Perspectives: Transformations in Environment and Society. https://doi.org/10.5282/rcc/8556.

McMichael, Philip. 2002. "La Restructuration Globale des Systems Agro-Alimentaires." *Mondes en Development* 30(117): 45–54.

2009. "A Food Regime Genealogy." *Journal of Peasant Studies* 36(1): 9–169.

McQuirter, Tracye. "By Any Greens Necessary." https://byanygreensnecessary.com/.

2010. *By Any Greens Necessary: A Revolutionary Guide for Black Women Who Want to Eat Great, Get Healthy, Lose Weight, and Look Phat.* New York: Lawrence Hill Books.

Meretoja, Hanna. 2018. *The Ethics of Storytelling: Narrative Hermeneutics, History, and the Possible.* Oxford: Oxford University Press.

Mitchell, Henry. 1986. *The Essential Earthman: Henry Mitchell on Gardening.* Bloomington: Indiana University Press.

Moloney, Kevin. 2014. "Multimedia, Crossmedia, Transmedia … What's in a Name?" *Transmedia Journalism* (April 21). https://transmediajournalism.org/2014/04/21/multimedia-crossmedia-transmedia-whats-in-a-name/.

Monani, Salma. 2013. "Indigenous Film Festival as Eco-testimonial Encounter – The 2011 Native Film + Video Festival." *NECSUS: European Journal of Media Studies* 2(1): 285–91.

Mosley, Della V., Helen A. Neville, Nayeli Y. Chavez-Dueñas, et al. 2020. "Radical Hope in Revolting Times: Proposing a Culturally Relevant Psychological Framework." *Social and Personality Psychology Compass* 14(1): e12512.

Murphy, Teagan and Anne Mook. 2022. "The Vegan Food Justice Movement." *The Palgrave Encyclopedia of Urban and Regional Futures*, edited by Robert C. Brears, 1–7. Basingstoke: Palgrave Macmillan.

Myers, Randy. 2021. "Revisiting the 'Occupy the Farm' doc: UC Berkeley farm saved in 2012 faces new threat." *Local News Matters* (April 13). https://

localnewsmatters.org/2021/04/13/revisiting-the-occupy-the-farm-doc-uc-berkeley-farm-saved-in-2012-faces-new-threat/.

Navarro, Marilisa C. 2021. "Radical Recipe: Veganism as Anti-Racism." In *The Routledge Handbook of Vegan Studies*, edited by Laura White, 282–293. New York: Routledge.

Nebraska Medicine. 2022. "What ASMR Means: How It Works and Why It's Popular." (April 26). www.nebraskamed.com/neurological-care/asmr-videos-are-exploding-online-but-what-is-asmr-and-does-it-work.

Neavling, Steve. 2021. "Detroit's Hantz Farms Is Beginning to Look Like a Land Grab After All." *Detroit Metro Times* (September 20). www.metrotimes.com/news/detroits-hantz-farms-is-beginning-to-look-like-a-land-grab-after-all-28100125.

NextBite Podcast. 2021. "Part 1: The Farm, with Germaine Jenkins of Fresh Future Farm." https://open.spotify.com/episode/4jDLOnQWtgnPiKRzmOXq6I?si=&nd=1&dlsi=929ce0ccc04b4adc.

Nichols, Bill. 2001. *Introduction to Documentary*. Bloomington, IN: Indiana University Press.

Nixon, Rob. 2011. *Slow Violence and the Environmentalism of the Poor*. Cambridge, MA: Harvard University Press.

O'Grady, Sean, dir. 2016. *Land Grab*. Atlas Industries.

Ojala, Maria. 2023. "Hope and Climate-change Engagement from a Psychological Perspective." *Current Opinion in Psychology* 49: 1–6. https://doi.org/10.1016/j.copsyc.2022.101514.

Quinn, Emilia. 2021. "Vegan Studies and Queer Theory." In *The Routledge Handbook of Vegan Studies*, edited by Laura White, 261–271. New York: Routledge.

Paddeu, Flaminia. 2017. "Legalising Urban Agriculture in Detroit: A Contested Way of Planning for Decline." *Town Planning Review* 88(1): 109–129. https://doi.org/10.3828/tpr.2017.9.

Painter, James. 2020. "A New Narrative." *UNA-UK Climate* 30–31. https://climate2020.org.uk/wp-content/uploads/2015/06/PAINTER-CLIMATE2020.pdf.

Paoletta, Kyle. 2023. "The Incredible Disappearing Doomsday." *Harper's Magazine* (April). https://harpers.org/archive/2023/04/the-incredible-disappearing-doomsday-climate-catastrophists-new-york-times-climate-change-coverage/.

Penniman, Leah. 2018. *Farming While Black*. White River Junction: Chelsea Green.

Pien, Diane. 2010. "Black Panther Party's Free Breakfast Program (1969–1980)." *Black Past* (February 11). www.blackpast.org/african-american-history/black-panther-partys-free-breakfast-program-1969-1980/.

Pihkala, Panu. 2022. "Toward a Taxonomy of Climate Emotions." *Frontiers in Climate* 3: 1–22. https://doi.org/10.3389/fclim.2021.738154.

Pinho, Kirk. 2021. "Hantz Quietly Sells off $2.8 million in Properties as Interest grows in Detroit Neighborhood." *Crain's Detroit Business* (September 21). www.crainsdetroi.com/real-estate/hantz-quietly-sells-28-million-properties-interest-grows-detroit-neighborhood.

Pirani, Daniela, and Ella Fegitz. 2019. "How Veggie Vlogging Looks Like: Intersections of Gender, Race, and Class in Western Mainstream Veganism." In *Feminist Food Studies: Intersectional Perspectives* edited by Barbara Parker, Jennifer Brady, Elaine Power, and Susan Belyea, 57–78. Toronto: Women's Press.

Plantinga, Carl. 2019. "Characterization and Character Engagement in the Documentary." In *Cognitive Theory and Documentary Film*, edited by Catalin Brylla and Mette Kramer, 115–132. Basingstoke: Palgrave Macmillan.

2023. "Introduction." In *Screen Stories and Moral Understanding: Interdisciplinary Perspectives*, edited by Carl Plantinga, 1–16, New York: Oxford University Press.

Poland, David. 2010. "*The Garden*, Documentarian Scott Hamilton Kennedy." *The Oral History of Hollywood*. www.youtube.com/watch?v=UrzdxgQXCb8.

Polish, Jennifer. 2016. "Decolonizing Veganism: On Resisting Vegan Whiteness and Racism." In *Critical Perspectives on Veganism*, edited by Jodey Castricano and Rasmus R. Simonsen, 273–291. Basingstoke: Palgrave Macmillan.

Polk, Eternal. 2023, dir. *Gaining Ground: The Fight for Black Land*. Blex Media.

Pollan, Michael. 1991. *Second Nature - A Gardener's Education*. New York: Atlantic Monthly Press.

2003. *Second Nature: A Gardener's Education*. New York: Grove Press.

Pothukuchi, Kameshwari. 2015. "Five Decades of Community Food Planning in Detroit: City and Grassroots, Growth and Equity." *Journal of Planning Education and Research* 35(4): 419–434.

Psihoyos, Louie, dir. 2018. *The Game Changers*. Ocean Preservation Society.

Queen Afua. 2001. *Sacred Woman: A Guide to Healing the Feminine Body, Mind, and Spirit*. New York: Random House.

Raneng, Jesse, Michael Howes, and Catherine Maria Pickering. 2023. "Current and Future Directions in Research on Community Gardens." *Urban Forestry & Urban Greening* 79. https://doi.org/10.1016/j.ufug.2022.127814.

Rawlins, Kimatni D. 2021. "Reprogramming the System." In *Brotha Vegan: Black Men Speak on Food, Identity, Health, and Society*, edited by Adewale, Omowale, 31–41. Brooklyn: Lantern.

Renov, Michael. 2008. "First-Person Films: Some Thoughts on Self-Inscription." *In Rethinking Documentary: New Perspectives, New Practices*, edited by Thomas Austin and Wilma de Jong, 29–50. Maidenhead: Open University Press.

Retzinger, Jean. 2011. "Eleven Miles South of Hollywood: Analyzing Narrative Strategies in *The Garden*." *Environmental Communication* 5(3): 337–343.

Reyes, Emily Alpert. 2019. "Latest Battle over South Central Farm Ends – This Time Not with Arrests, but a Vote." *Los Angeles Times* (July 2). www .latimes.com/local/lanow/la-me-ln-south-central-farm-alameda-industrial-businesses-20190702-story.html.

Roeder, Tara. 2021. "Beyond Diet: Veganism as Liberatory Praxis." In *Veg(etari) an Arguments in Culture, History, and Practice: The V Word*." edited by Cristina Hanganu-Bresch and Kristin Kondrlik, 291–318. Basingstoke: Palgrave Macmillan.

Roman-Alcalá, Antonio. 2017. "Occupy the Farm: The Legitimacy of Direct Action to Create Land Commons." In *Land Justice: Re-imagining Land, Food, and the Commons*, edited by Justine M. Williams and Eric Holt-Giménez, 260–272. Oakland, CA: Food First Books.

Romm, Cari. 2015. "What 'Food Porn' Does to the Brain: What's the Psychological Appeal of Looking at Food that Can't be Tasted?" *The Atlantic* (April 20). www.theatlantic.com/health/archive/2015/04/what-food-porn-does-to-the-brain/390849/?utm_source=SFTwitter.

Ryan, Marie-Laure. 2004. *Narrative Across Media: The Languages of Storytelling*. Lincoln: University of Nebraska Press.

Santosa, Melissa. 2010. "Identity, Freedom, and Veganism." In *Sistah Vegan: Black Female Vegans Speak on Food, Identity, Health, and Society*, edited by A. Breeze Harper, 73–77. New York: Lantern.

Sargent, Lyman Tower. 2019. "From Production to Disposal: The Interaction of Food and Society in Utopias." In *Utopian Foodways: Critical Essays*, edited by Teresa Botelho, Miguel Ramalhete Gomes, and José Eduardo Reis, 15–31. Porto: University of Porto Press.

Sbicca, Joshua. 2018. *Food Justice Now! Deepening the Roots of Social Struggle*. Minneapolis: University of Minnesota Press.

Schmid Callina, Kristina, Nancy Snow, and Elise D. Murray. 2018. "The History of Philosophical and Psychological Perspectives on Hope." In *The Oxford Handbook of Hope*, edited by Mattew W. Gallagher and Shane J. Lopez, 9–25. New York: Oxford University Press.

Schneider-Mayerson, Matthew, Alexa Weik von Mossner, W. P. Malecki, and Frank Hakemulder, eds. 2023. *Empirical Ecocriticism: Environmental Narratives for Social Change*. Minneapolis: University of Minnesota Press.

Schüssler, Petra, Michael Kluge, Alexander Yassouridis et al. 2012. "Ghrelin Levels Increase after Pictures Showing Food." *Obesity* 20(6): 1212–1217.

Scoop, Sarah. 2021. "Jasmine C. Leyva, *The Invisible Vegan*." *SarahScoop. com*. www.youtube.com/watch?v=PFc6HzeO0vw.

Shah, Khushbu. 2018. "The Vegan Race Wars: How the Mainstream Ignores Vegans of Color." *Thrillist* (January 26). www.thrillist.com/eat/nation/ vegan-race-wars-white-veganism.

Smith, Murray. 2021. *Engaging Characters: Fiction, Emotion, and the Cinema.* 2nd ed. New York: Oxford University Press.

　2022. *Engaging Characters: Fiction, Emotion, and the Cinema.* New York: Oxford University Press.

Smithsonian Gardens. 2024. "Grown from the Past: A Short History of Community Gardening in the United States." https://communityofgar dens.si.edu/exhibits/show/historycommunitygardens/intro.

Smith-Tran, Alicia. 2020. "Review of *The Invisible Vegan* by Jasmine Leyva and Kenny Levya." *Teaching Sociology* 48(4): 373–375.

SNCC Digital Gateway. n.d. "Fannie Lou Hamer founds Freedom Farm Cooperative." https://snccdigital.org/events/fannie-lou-hamer-founds-free dom-farm-cooperative/.

Spiegel, Marjorie. 1996. *The Dreaded Comparison: Human and Animal Slavery.* New York: Mirror Books.

Stahler, Charles, and Reed Mangels. 2022. "Adult Poll: How Many Adults in the U.S. Are Vegan and Vegetarian?" *The Vegetarian Resource Group.* www .vrg.org/nutshell/faq.htm#poll.

Starkman, Naomi. 2009. "*The Garden*: A Film, A Call to Action." *Civil Eats* (May 11). https://civileats.com/2009/05/11/the-garden-a-film-a-call-to-action/.

Stock, Paul V., Michael Carolan, and Christopher Rosin. 2015. *Food Utopias: Reimagining Citizenship, Ethics and Community.* New York: Routledge.

Strazds, Laila M. 2019. "Radical Hope: Transforming Sustainability." *Journal of Sustainability Education* 21. www.susted.com/wordpress/content/rad ical-hope-transforming-sustainability_2019_12/.

Stuckey, Barb. 2012. *Taste: Surprising Stories and Science about Why Food Tastes Good.* New York: Atria.

Sulimma, Maria. 2023. "'I Am Not by Any Stretch a Gardener, Just Curious': Feminist Gentrifier Memoirs and an Ethics of Urban Gardening." *Ecozon@: European Journal of Literature, Culture, and Environment* 14(1): 70–86.

Susman, Dan, dir. 2013. *Growing Cities.* Elmwood Motion Picture.

Tarlau, Rebecca. 2012. "Putting the Gill Tract Occupation in an International Context." *Albany Patch* (May 2008). http://albany.patch.com/articles/col umn-putting-the-gill-tract-occupation-in-an-international-context.

Terry, Bryant. 2009. *Vegan Soul Kitchen: Fresh, Healthy, and Creative African-American Cuisine*. Cambridge, MA: Da Capo Press.

2012. *The Inspired Vegan: Seasonal Ingredients, Creative Recipes, Mouthwatering Menus*. Cambridge, MA: Da Capo Press.

2014. *Afro-Vegan: Farm-Fresh African, Caribbean, and Southern Flavors Remixed*. Berkeley: Ten Speed Press.

Terry, Bryant, ed. 2021. *Black Food: Stories, Art & Recipes from Across the African Diaspora*. Berkeley: Ten Speed Press.

Terry, Bryant, prod. 2023. "Sustenance and Liberation." *Bryant Terry Website*. www.bryant-terry.com/art.

Thomason, Krista. 2020. "The Moral Necessity of Anger." In *The Ethics of Anger*, edited by Court D. Lewis and Gregory L. Bock, 83–102. Lanham, Mayland: Lexington.

Thon, Jan-Noël. 2016. *Transmedial Narratology and Contemporary Culture*. Lincoln: University of Nebraska Press.

Turshen, Julia. 2018. "To Change Racial Disparity in Food, Let's Start with Cookbooks." *Eater* (April 5). www.eater.com/2018/4/5/17153806/racial-inequality-food-cookbook-authors-publishing.

van Laer, Tom, and Davide Orazi. 2023. "Narrative Agency." *Journal of the Association for Consumer Research* 9(1).

Vegan Geography Collective. 2024. "Justice for All? Expanding Questions and Spaces of (In)Justice through Multispecies Research, Teaching and Activism." In *Researching Justice*, edited by Agatha Herman and Joshua Inwood, 139–158. Bristol: Bristol University Press.

Véron, Ophélie. 2016. "From Seitan Bourguignon to Tofu Blanquette: Popularizing Veganism in France with Food Blogs." In *Critical Perspectives on Veganism*, edited by Jodey Catricano and Rasmus R. Simonsen, 287–306. Baskingstoke: Palgrave Macmillan.

Videle, Jimmy. 2022. *The Veganic Grower's Handbook: Cultivating Fruits, Vegetables and Herbs from Urban Backyard to Rural Farmyard*. New York: Lantern.

Vitiello, D. and Laura Wolf-Powers. 2014. "Growing Food to Grow Cities? The Potential of Agriculture for Economic and Community Development in the Urban United States." *Community Development Journal* 49(4): 508–552. https://doi.org/10.1093/cdj/bst087.

Wald, Nave. 2015. "Towards Utopias of Prefigurative Politics and Food Sovereignty: Experiences of Politicised Peasant Food Production." In *Food*

Utopias: Reimagining Citizenship, Ethics and Community, edited by Paul V. Stock, Michael Carolan, and Christopher Rosin, 107–124. New York: Routledge.

Walker, Jo. 2023. "'Food Desert' vs. 'Food Apartheid': Which Term Best Describes Disparities in Food Access?" (November 29). *University of Michigan School for Environment and Sustainability*. https://seas.umich.edu/news/food-desert-vs-food-apartheid-which-term-best-describes-disparities-food-access.

Weik von Mossner, Alexa. 2017. *Affective Ecologies: Empathy, Emotion and Environmental Narrative*. Columbus: Ohio State University Press.

2019. "How We Feel about (Not) Eating Animals: Vegan Studies and Cognitive Ecocriticism." In *Through a Vegan Studies Lens: Textual Ethics and Lived Activism*, edited by Laura White, 28–47. Lincoln: University of Nevada Press.

Widener, Michael J. 2018. "Spatial Access to Food: Retiring the Food Desert Metaphor." *Physiology & Behavior* 193(Part B): 257–260.

Wheeler, Tim, and Joachim von Braun. 2013. "Climate Change Impacts on Global Food Security." *Science* 341(508). https://doi.org/10.1126/science.1239402.

White, Courtney. 2020. "Why Regenerative Agriculture?" *The American Journal of Economics and Sociology* 3: 799–812.

White, Erik Olin. 2007. "Guidelines for Envisioning Real Utopias." *Soundings* 36: 26–39.

White, Monica M. 2011. "Sisters of the Soil: Urban Gardening as Resistance in Detroit." *Race/Ethnicity: Multidisciplinary Global Contexts* 5(1): 13–28.

2018. *Freedom Farmers: Agricultural Resistance and the Black Freedom Movement*. Chapel Hill: University of North Carolina Press.

Witt, Doris. 1999. *Black Hunger: Food and the Politics of US Identity*. Oxford: Oxford University Press.

Wittman, Hannah, Annette Desmarais, and Nettie Wiebe. 2010. "Seeing Like a Peasant: The Origins of Food Sovereignty." In *Food Sovereignty: Reconnecting Food, Nature and Community*, edited by H. Wittman, A. A. Desmarais and N. Wiebe. Winnipeg: Fernwood.

Woods, Nicole, and Julie M. Turner-Cobb. 2023. "'It's like Taking a Sleeping Pill': Student Experience of Autonomous Sensory Meridian Response (ASMR) to Promote Health and Mental Wellbeing." *International Journal of Environmental Research and Public Health* 20(3): 2337.

Womack, Ytasha. 2013. *Afrofuturism: The World of Black Sci-fi and Fantasy Culture*. Chicago: Chicago Review Press.

Woo, Elaine. 2004. "Juanita Tate, 66; South L.A. Community Activist." *Los Angeles Times* (July 8). www.latimes.com/archives/la-xpm-2004-jul-08-me-tate8-story.html.

World Food Programme. 2024. *WFP Global Operational Response Plan: Update #11 – June 2024.* www.wfp.org/publications/wfp-global-oper ational-response-plan.

Wright, Laura. 2015. *The Vegan Studies Project: Food, Animals, and Gender in the Age of Terror.* Athens: University of Georgia Press.

2017. "Introducing Vegan Studies." *ISLE: Interdisciplinary Studies in Literature and Environment* 24(4), 727–736. https://doi.org/10.1093/isle/ isx070.

2019. "Doing Vegan Studies: An Introduction." In *Through a Vegan Studies Lens: Textual Ethics and Lived Activism*, edited by Laura Wright, vii–xxiv. Reno: University of Nevada Press.

Zhang, Yujia, Jordan P. Smith, Daoqin Tong, and B. L. Turner II. 2022. "Optimizing the Co-benefits of Food Desert and Urban Heat Mitigation through Community Garden Planning." *Landscape and Urban Planning* 226, 104488. https://doi.org/10.1016/j.landurbplan.2022.104488.

Acknowledgments

My great thanks go out to so many friends and colleagues who have inspired and supported me on my journey to *Growing Hope*: To the scholars in the fields of ecocriticism, food justice studies, and vegan studies, whose work has been so inspiring. To Wojciech Malecki, Matthew Schneider-Mayerson, Marcus Mayorga, and Paul Slovic, who collaborated with me on a reception study on Alice Walker's "Am I Blue?" which raised some of the issues that inform my analysis here. I also want to thank Frederick Luis Aldama, Jim Donahue, Jennifer Ho, Matthias Klestil, Marijana Mikić, Derek Maus, and Paula Moya for helping me think about narrative in relation to critical race studies. To the colleagues and students whose comments on my presentations of various parts of *Growing Hope* have been extremely helpful. To Neil Osborne for opening my eyes to the transmedial aspect of nonfiction narratives. To Mirabai Collins, for inviting me to visit the Black Future Farm in Portland, Oregon, and giving me so much insight into what it means to successfully run a community garden. To Timo Maran, Serenella Iovino, and Louise Westling as editors of the Cambridge Elements in Environmental Humanities series for their immediate interest in my topic and the great collaboration during the entire publication process. To the English Department at the University of Klagenfurt for granting me a sabbatical so I could finish this project. To Evi Zemanek for inviting me to be a visiting professor in the Institute for Media and Cultural Studies at the University of Freiburg and for encouraging me to teach a class there based on *Growing Hope*. And to the students in that class, whose many brilliant comments and ideas helped me think about the project in new ways.

As always, I want to thank my family for their love and support and my husband, Michael, without whom nothing I have done over the past two decades would have been possible.

Cambridge Elements ≡

Environmental Humanities

Louise Westling
University of Oregon

Louise Westling is an American scholar of literature and environmental humanities who was a founding member of the Association for the Study of Literature and Environment and its President in 1998 She has been active in the international movement for environmental cultural studies, teaching and writing on landscape imagery in literature, critical animal studies, biosemiotics, phenomenology, and deep history.

Serenella Iovino
University of North Carolina at Chapel Hill

Serenella Iovino is Professor of Italian Studies and Environmental Humanities at the University of North Carolina at Chapel Hill. She has written on a wide range of topics, including environmental ethics and ecocritical theory, bioregionalism and landscape studies, ecofeminism and posthumanism, comparative literature, eco-art, and the Anthropocene.

Timo Maran
University of Tartu

Timo Maran is an Estonian semiotician and poet. Maran is Professor of Ecosemiotics and Environmental Humanities and Head of the Department of Semiotics at the University of Tartu. His research interests are semiotic relations of nature and culture, Estonian nature writing, zoosemiotics and species conservation, and semiotics of biological mimicry.

About the Series

The environmental humanities is a new transdisciplinary complex of approaches to the embeddedness of human life and culture in all the dynamics that characterize the life of the planet. These approaches reexamine our species' history in light of the intensifying awareness of drastic climate change and ongoing mass extinction. To engage this reality, Cambridge Elements in Environmental Humanities builds on the idea of a more hybrid and participatory mode of research and debate, connecting critical and creative fields.

For EU product safety concerns, contact us at Calle de José Abascal, 56–1°,
28003 Madrid, Spain or eugpsr@cambridge.org.